Blood in the Face

Blood in the Face

The Ku Klux Klan, Aryan Nations, Nazi Skinheads, and the Rise of a New White Culture

by James Ridgeway

Thunder's Mouth Press

New York

Published by Thunder's Mouth Press

First edition.
92 93 94 95 96/9 8 7 6 5 4 3

Library of Congress Cataloging-in-Publication data:

Ridgeway, James, 1936-
    Blood in the face: the Ku Klux Klan, Aryan Nations, Nazi
    skinheads, and the rise of a new white culture / by James Ridgeway
    — 1st ed.
        p.   cm.
    ISBN 1-56025-002-X: $29.95. — ISBN 1-56025-003-8 (pbk.): $18.95
    1. White supremacy movements — United States.   2. United States —
    Race relations.   I. Title.
E184.A1R482   1990
305.8'00973 — dc20

90-10921
CIP

Portions of the text of this book were originally published in the *Village Voice*. Reprinted by permission of the author and the *Village Voice*.

Grateful acknowledgment is made to the following institutions for providing materials for this book: Illustration from the *Protocols of the Elders of Zion* courtesy of the American Jewish Committee, Blaustein Library. Frontispiece from *The Clansman* courtesy of Grosset & Dunlap Publishers, Inc. Documents by Gerald L.K. Smith courtesy of the Wilcox Collection, University of Kansas Libraries. Photographs of 1989 rallies in Pulaski, TN and Gainesville, GA courtesy of the Center for Democratic Renewal. Photograph of Glenn Miller courtesy of the Southern Poverty Law Center. Burning cross photo on contents page by Charlie Arnot.

Text design by Ed Hedemann.

Typeset by Royal Type.

Manufactured in the United States of America.

Contents

Preface

As Ronald Reagan's campaign cavalcade advanced through Illinois on a lovely autumn day in 1980, time seemed to stand still. The TV images were picture perfect: In every town, along the downtown streets, knots of people gathered. Well-scrubbed youngsters clutching American flags rode atop their fathers' shoulders. High school bands and city officials waited in growing excitement for the candidate to appear. Then, out of nowhere, he was there — police lights whirling, squinty-eyed Secret Service agents running alongside the limousines, a chopper hovering overhead. And in the midst of this travelling cocoon was Ronald Reagan: serene, confident, ready to usher in a new era that would be symbolized by the images of the past — of small-town America with its time-honored and cherished values and traditions.

Four years later, during the height of the farm depression, I once again travelled across the Midwest, reporting on the presidential campaign between the then–solidly ensconced and popular Reagan and the Democratic challenger Walter Mondale. Nothing in the scheduled formal campaign appearances or debates had prepared me for the world I encountered. America's heartland showed itself to be a never-never land of desperate people: Farm families that had homesteaded land for more than a century were going broke. Shop-owners were working as gas station attendants, farm wives as maids. Small-town businesses were shuttered, stores on Main Street empty.

In that transformed world of the American heartland, the Republican and Democratic parties had become abstractions. It was a world of fervent and unexpected beliefs — where Ronald Reagan was considered a pathetic pawn of the eastern bankers and George Bush an active agent of the Trilateral Commission; where Texas agriculture commissioner Jim Hightower became the Lone Ranger of a nationwide populist front for taking a stand against agri-business on behalf of the small farmer; where arch-liberal George McGovern stood resurrected as a plains hero; where the whacko candidates of Lyndon LaRouche's party were serious contenders; and where veteran civil rights activist Jesse Jackson repeatedly brought farmers to their feet in foot-stomping excitement.

But for the most part, it was a world where hope came from the right — surprisingly, not from Ronald Reagan's electorally successful New Right revolution, but from the racist far right, the "lunatic fringe." It was the leadership of barnstorming hucksters on the far right that urged the farmers to fight back. As Democrats and Republicans, liberals and conservatives watched from the sidelines, such groups as the Posse Comitatus counselled these farmers to go into court without lawyers, and to file elaborate, arcane legal proceedings aimed at stalling farm foreclosures. And when the bankers and the judges held against the farmers anyway, adherents of the far right mocked the auctioneers, holding up single dollars as bids, in some cases chasing the bankers and sheriffs from the podiums in angry acts of resistance. More importantly, the far right provided small-town America with an interpretive framework with which to understand what was taking place: the purported "hidden truth" behind the nightmare chaos of the times. For example, behind the farm depression in the Midwest, the outriders of the racist right argued, was a carefully orchestrated worldwide Jewish conspiracy emanating from Moscow, with ties to the Federal Reserve. In tracts, meetings, recorded phone messages, and publications, white revolutionary groups addressed the fear and anger of a large and growing group of Americans who felt that conventional political options offered no hope.

It has been commonplace to dismiss such ideas of the racist far right as an aberration on the paranoid fringe of American life. But both the political ideas and the culture of this far-right revolution have roiled just below the surface of the conservative riptide, and today remain disconcertingly close to mainstream politics.

This book sets out to trace the evolution of the racialist right in American politics. It aims to explain the historical developments which led to contemporary far-right ideology. The progress of the political culture is treated chronologically: The book begins with the origins of the myth of the international Jewish conspiracy, traces the history of the Ku Klux Klan and other groups, and surveys the many players in today's racialist far right.

In addition, this book aims to let the culture of the far right speak for itself, in the writings, sermons, last words, statements, cartoons, and screeds of its participants, so that this political and cultural phenomenon can be examined directly. With the news media focusing only on the more violent or sensational aspects of racialist white revolutionary politics, what has gone largely unnoticed and unrecorded is the actual substance of what is a surprisingly enduring and resourceful movement. What this book attempts to do is examine the organizational histories, personalities, and home-grown statements of a movement which, though developed in semi-secrecy, increasingly demands to be reckoned with by everyone living in a racially polarized America.

Acknowledgments

This book grew out of my reporting on the far right for the *Village Voice*, which has consistently supported my work over the last decade. The project also owes a special debt to Anne Bohlen and Kevin Rafferty, my partners in the making of a documentary film about the far right in contemporary America, also called *Blood in the Face*. One of the aims of this book is to complement and provide a context for the film. I also am indebted to Michael Moore and to Charlie Arnot, who played important roles in the making of the film.

Kristine Jacobs first persuaded me to begin reporting on the far right, and I am especially grateful for her help and advice. Leonard Zeskind and Daniel Levitas of the Center for Democratic Renewal, the staff of the Klanwatch project at the Southern Poverty Law Center (especially Randall Williams and Danny Welch), and Wes McCune at Group Research have provided me with information and assistance over the years, and I am grateful for their help in preparing the book. Lance Hill provided research assistance for the sections on David Duke. Mark Ritchie, Merle Hanson, Darrell Ringer, and the members of Prairiefire and the League of Rural Voters took the time to teach me about the politics and culture of the American Midwest. Gerry Gable and the staff of *Searchlight* helped me to understand the complexities of the far right in Europe.

Dan Bischoff, my editor at the *Village Voice*, gave me sound advice and was of great assistance in editing the manuscript. Ed Hedemann designed the book and also made invaluable contributions to the editing process. I want to thank my associates at the *Village Voice*: Lisa Hubbard did the picture research; and Bill Gifford, Jeremiah Drake, and Leslie Conner all helped me find material, did reporting, and ran down documents. Dallas Galvin kindly made translations from the European press. Philip Levy helped me find resource materials for the project. Denny Whelan, Irv Nodland, Frank Browning, Byron Foster, Dan Gilmore, and Judge Sam Van Pelt assisted greatly with my research on the Posse Comitatus. Marcia Ogrodnik also helped me at various stages of the research.

This book could never have been done without the support of Neil Ortenberg and the staff of Thunder's Mouth Press. I want to thank Jean Casella, who patiently shepherded the manuscript along the road to publication; Michael Schwartz for his expert editing and criticism; Rachel Straus and Eliza C. Galaher for their last-minute research and proofreading; and Anne Stillwaggon, Marjorie

Laue, Eric Brandt and Janey Tannenbaum for their behind-the-scenes work in organizing the production and promotion.

I owe a special debt to the reporters and historians who over the last decade have taken a fresh look at the far right and its implications for American culture and history. Chief among these are Leo Ribuffo, whose book on the old Christian right provides a thorough exploration of the foundations of the current movement, and Glen Jeansonne, Wyn Craig Wade, James Corcoran, Kevin Flynn, Gary Gerhardt, and James Coates, who have all shed light on the history and ramifications of the far right. In addition, Wayne King's reportage on the far right in the *New York Times* supplied me with an almost daily summary of what was unfolding in the American heartland during the early 1980s.

Finally, I gained an added understanding of the politics and culture of the far right through various interviews, and most importantly by attending two different meetings at Bob Miles's Michigan farm. My film colleagues and I went at his invitation, and as a result were able to interview and film the participants in the movement, from leadership to ordinary members. While neither I nor my partners agree with the far-right view of history, Miles and his associates politely answered our questions, even when they probably thought, in the end, that we were undercover agents of some police force.

J.R.
August 1990

Blood in the Face

Tight, Right, & White

Forced off a narrow, winding country road north of San Francisco, the driver of the Brinks armored truck found himself staring at a hand-lettered sign that was stuck up in front of the windshield: "Get out or die." Behind layers of bulletproof glass, driver and guard sat nervously. Suddenly a man clambored up on the front fender and, raising an automatic weapon, aimed at the windshield. Without hesitation he opened fire.

By counterfeiting, violent robberies, and murder, an armed gang known to newspaper readers as the Order blazed its way into the American consciousness during the mid-1980s. It was a white gang, and it robbed and plundered not only to make money for money's sake, but to raise funds for a revolutionary movement to establish a new whites-only homeland in the Pacific Northwest — a "White Bastion." And these sensational events were only the tip of an iceberg, for beyond the Order lay a political movement that had been dormant for over a decade. Now it was on the move.

One might have thought that political battles centered on race issues ended with the victories of the civil rights movement during the 1960s. But recently,

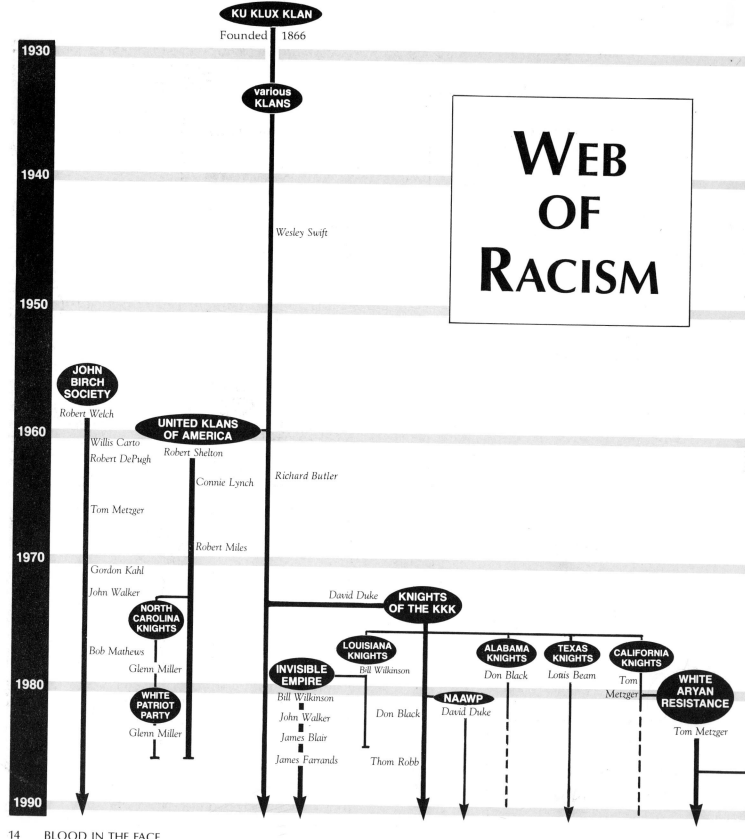

KU KLUX KLAN
Founded 1866

various KLANS

Wesley Swift

WEB OF RACISM

1930
1940
1950
1960
1970
1980
1990

JOHN BIRCH SOCIETY
Robert Welch

Willis Carto
Robert DePugh

Tom Metzger

Gordon Kahl

John Walker

Bob Mathews

Glenn Miller

WHITE PATRIOT PARTY
Glenn Miller

UNITED KLANS OF AMERICA
Robert Shelton

Connie Lynch

Robert Miles

NORTH CAROLINA KNIGHTS

Richard Butler

David Duke

KNIGHTS OF THE KKK

INVISIBLE EMPIRE
Bill Wilkinson
John Walker
James Blair
James Farrands

LOUISIANA KNIGHTS
Bill Wilkinson

Don Black

Thom Robb

NAAWP
David Duke

ALABAMA KNIGHTS
Don Black

TEXAS KNIGHTS
Louis Beam

CALIFORNIA KNIGHTS
Tom Metzger

WHITE ARYAN RESISTANCE
Tom Metzger

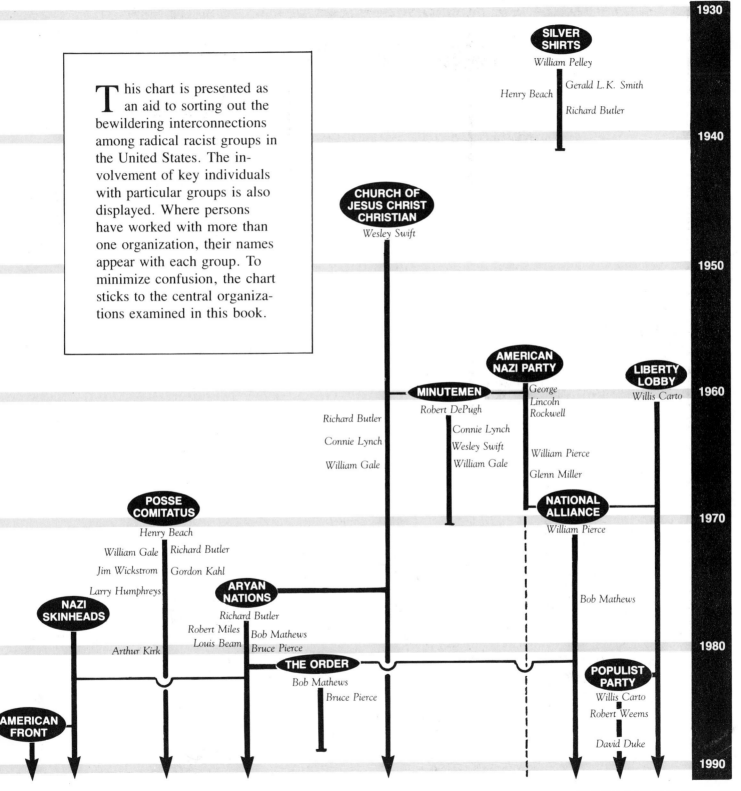

This chart is presented as an aid to sorting out the bewildering interconnections among radical racist groups in the United States. The involvement of key individuals with particular groups is also displayed. Where persons have worked with more than one organization, their names appear with each group. To minimize confusion, the chart sticks to the central organizations examined in this book.

1930

SILVER SHIRTS
William Pelley

Henry Beach   Gerald L.K. Smith
              Richard Butler

1940

CHURCH OF JESUS CHRIST CHRISTIAN
Wesley Swift

1950

AMERICAN NAZI PARTY

MINUTEMEN   **LIBERTY LOBBY**
                    Willis Carto

Robert DePugh   George
                     Lincoln
Richard Butler   Rockwell   **1960**

Connie Lynch   Connie Lynch

William Gale   Wesley Swift   William Pierce
                 William Gale   Glenn Miller

POSSE COMITATUS   **NATIONAL ALLIANCE**
                                 William Pierce   **1970**
Henry Beach

William Gale   Richard Butler

Jim Wickstrom   Gordon Kahl   Bob Mathews

Larry Humphreys

ARYAN NATIONS

NAZI SKINHEADS

                Richard Butler

           Robert Miles   Bob Mathews
Arthur Kirk   Louis Beam Bruce Pierce   **1980**

THE ORDER

AMERICAN FRONT   Bob Mathews   **POPULIST PARTY**
                     Bruce Pierce   Willis Carto
                                       Robert Weems

                                       David Duke

                                                    1990

BLOOD IN THE FACE   15

racially inspired hostility and fear have become a staple topic on television, and race continues to shape the way we live and think. In 1988, race was made a defining issue of the presidential election. The Democratic Party conducted an internal pitched battle over the role of a black man running for president, and in the Republican Party deft professionals employed racial stereotypes and fears as a major device for attracting young, white male voters. Race largely defines our political discourse, shaping unspoken assumptions in the arguments over U.S. immigration even as the complexion of our population changes. As it has for generations, race continues to play a large part in defining the rights of our citizens, and influencing who can vote, which women are permitted to have abortions, whether a young man goes to jail.

But beyond the racialist impulses shaping American society, there are political forces with what to many would seem arcane racial goals, aimed at turning the nation back to a starkly segregated past. This political agenda is often hidden from view.

This book is about that movement and its effect on our wider political culture. Since the Second World War, anti-communism has been the glue that bound American political culture together. Whether it was the Cold War politics of the Democratic Party or the patriotic rhetoric of the different, often squabbling groups that made up the Reagan revolution, opposition to the godless Red menace was the touchstone that sanctified their common goals and shared ideals for the future. But now, with communism on the wane both as fact and idea, the old, enduring force is once again moving, with unexpected intensity, to the center of American political life: Race politics.

Beginning with the Goldwater debacle in 1964, the American right-wing underwent a sea change, re-emerging in 1980 as Reagan's New Right. It was an uneasy coalition that generally consisted of older, long-time conservatives who had supported Goldwater; southern and midwestern Protestant fundamentalists who had deserted the Democratic Party to support George Wallace; and Libertarians, the supply-side free marketeers who rallied around Jack Kemp. These factions have been at odds on a number of fundamental issues — the religious right, for example, supports efforts by the state to regulate social behavior, while the supply-sider libertarians oppose state intervention wherever possible. But their shared opposition to

It is simple reality that...

To be born WHITE is an honor and a privilege

WAR

communism papered over most of their differences, at least at first.

These new conservatives are not racists, although, as with the Goldwater movement of the 1960s, racists may dwell under the New Right tent. Their support for Israel, for one thing, has forever set them apart from the racialist far right. But riding on the wave of the New Right coalition was also a diverse group of right-wing anarchists, Nazis, splinter groups of the Ku Klux Klan, and so-called Constitutionalists who had come together briefly and tenuously in the Goldwater campaign, then later in George Wallace's 1968 campaign for the presidency. In recent years the movement has been further propelled by young skinheads and out-of-work white youths worldwide, who have given the racists a truly internationalist tone for the first time. In the 1980s, these groups evolved into both an above-ground political movement — utilizing electoral politics, lawsuits, and talk show appearances — and, sporadically, a violent underground.

Ku Klux Klan

The Roots of the Racist Right

The theoretical underpinnings for today's far right originated at the time of the French Revolution in the creation of the myth of an "international Jewish conspiracy." Evolving and expanding over the years, this myth worked its way through Europe in the early twentieth century, and was popularized in America during the 1920s, when fear and antagonism towards immigrants and naturalized aliens was at its height. Automobile tycoon Henry Ford was one of the first and most influential promulgators of the doctrine of an international Jewish conspiracy; and the idea was taken up by the burgeoning Ku Klux Klan, and added to its already busy agenda of anti-black and anti-Catholic terror.

The myth gained currency with the addition of a quasi-theological theory called Christian Identity, which held that the Anglo-Saxons were the Lost Tribe of Israel and that Jews, blacks, and other people of color were inferiors sent to earth as a scourge of God. At the coming of the Apocalypse, Identity followers believe, the earth will be rid of these "mud people," and reserved for the only true Israelite people: white Aryans, whose sign of racial purity is their ability to blush, to have "blood in the face."

An additional strain running through racialist theory in America has been nativism, a cultural movement that drew its central impulse from an opposition to all things foreign. Racist right-wing movements have been traditionally linked to nativism, featuring hatred of immigrant groups, calls

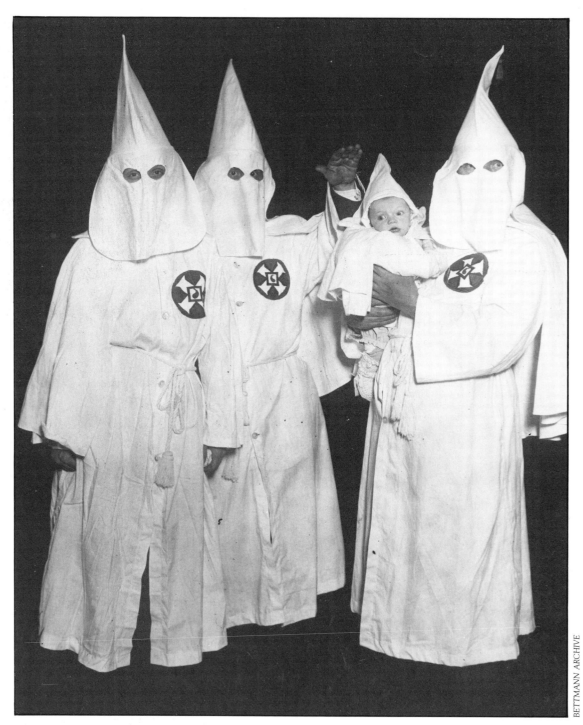

Ku Klux Klansmen with infant at a secret night meeting in the early 1920s.

for a closing of U.S. borders, and support of strict adherence to the Constitution in its most literal sense, shorn of equivocating amendments, as a remedy for unwanted social change.

The origins of many of today's far-right movements can be traced back to the tumultuous politics of the 1930s, and recognized clearly in the political career of Gerald L.K. Smith. Beginning as a mainstream Protestant minister, influenced by progressive and populist political movements, Smith became the national organizer for then–Louisiana Senator Huey Long's populist "Share Our Wealth" campaign. When Long was assassinated in 1935, Smith vied briefly with other Louisiana politicians to take over his machine, and then set off on his own populist — and, increasingly, racialist — crusade.

Smith's followers also had links to organizations which spawned the leadership of new racialist white revolutionary groups. One such figure was Wesley Swift, a Christian Identity minister of the Church of Jesus Christ Christian in California. Swift's church was a meeting ground for a group of men who went on to become leaders of various factions in the far-right political movement. Among Swift's parishioners was Richard Butler, a former aircraft executive who built a Christian Identity church and compound in Hayden Lake, Idaho. Hayden Lake became a mecca for the racist far right, and the headquarters of the Aryan Nations. Attached to the Aryan Nations was the violent underground splinter group called the Order. Another Swift follower was William Gale, a staff aide to General Douglas MacArthur during World War II who went on to set up his own paramilitary operation called the California Rangers. In 1969 Gale would set up a chapter of yet another far-right group, the Posse Comitatus.

Gerald L.K. Smith provided the connecting

Aryan Nations

link between pre–World War II protest movements on the far right and organizations such as the Posse Comitatus, the Aryan Nations, and the Ku Klux Klan, which helped comprise the racist far right of the 1980s. Smith himself sputtered on at the fringe of American politics until his death in 1976. Although he was a gifted political promoter, fund raiser, and speaker, he lacked an enduring and broad-based constituency after his initial success in post–Huey Long Louisiana. But his political legacy is the development of the organizations founded by his followers — organizations which became the major elements of the resurgent white resistance movement of the 1980s.

"Old-Fashioned American Justice"

Two contemporary organizations that can be viewed as mainstays of the far-right political movement are the Ku Klux Klan and the Posse Comitatus. The Klan, since its inception, has undergone successive periods of expansion and decline. Its First Era, during post–Civil War radical reconstruction, saw an insurgent outlaw army. It soon withered, then rose again in a Second Era in the 1920s, an above-ground political phase that attracted millions of members. The Third Era was a violent, rear-guard battle against the civil rights movement of the 1960s. The Fourth Era, in the 1970s, was a public relations campaign, led most importantly by the young David Duke, who would go on to become a member of the Louisiana state legislature and, in 1990, make a run for the U.S. Senate. The Fifth Era, in the 1980s and beyond, involves both an armed underground and an aggressive aboveboard political movement. Over the years, the Klans' attacks on blacks have been augmented by a preoccupation with Asians and other immigrants,

Posse Comitatus

Jews, and communists. Its infamous episodes of night riding and lynching have made way for public demonstrations and forays into mainstream party politics, as well as the formation of ties with other right-wing factions.

A second prominent organization, the Posse Comitatus, was formed in Portland, Oregon in the late 1960s. Posse doctrine is based on the idea that the local sheriff is the supreme governmental figure and that he should exercise authority in his territory — the county — unrestrained by state or federal officials. The Posse cleaves to strongly nativist sensibilities, arguing that the U.S. Constitution prohibits the collection of federal income tax, that the Federal Reserve is part of an international banking plot, and that the U.S. should adopt a strict isolationist policy in world affairs. The Posse seems to hold special appeal among the midwestern farm families who are losing their farms to government and bank foreclosures. While the most noteworthy exponents of Posse thinking are racialists such as Jim Wickstrom, a Christian Identity preacher, not everyone who subscribes to Posse ideas is a racist. Posse ideology appeals to a variety of different groups, whose names change from year to year. Many members are small-town, mainstream Republicans who believe the nation has gone too far down the road to socialism and world government, and who are likely to have earlier joined the John Birch Society. Others subscribe to a kind of rugged survivalism, and may have belonged to paramilitary groups such as the Minutemen. Likewise, the activities of Posse members range from party politics to income tax evasion to murder. One of Jim Wickstrom's Posse bulletins features a drawing of a lynching with the banner, "It's time for old-fashioned American Justice."

The Klan and the Posse Comitatus are far

Members of the SS Action Team from Detroit at a gathering of the radical right at Bob Miles's Michigan farm in 1986.

from the only elements in the revolutionary white racialist far right. As with any political movement, there are and have been many organizations of varying size and longevity that have exercised influence on the movement's ideological direction. In the 1960s, for example, the American Nazi Party experienced a brief revival under the leadership of George Lincoln Rockwell. In the early 1980s, the Order blazed across the scene. And recently, the nebulous but growing skinhead movement has developed into an international phenomenon.

Leaders of the New Far Right

The interconnections among these organizations and the growth of a broad-based far-right movement can be better understood by examining some key individuals whose activities cut across organizational lines. In the 1980s three men, all one-time members of the Klan, provided the rising movement with the theoretician, the politician, and the youth leader it needed to create a functional program of national racist politics.

As a theoretician, Bob Miles has articulated the battleground of white revolution in the 1970s and 1980s, supporting various forms of protest and leading the search for a separate white bastion, a home in which the "disintegrating" Aryan people might recover their lost moorings. In knitting together a movement and providing it with an ideo-

JEW BUSTERS

WHITE ARYAN RESISTANCE

P O BOX 54065
TULSA OK 74155   (918) 627-0818

logical and tactical framework, Miles has sought to promote what he called the Fifth Era Klan. From a small rural community outside Flint, Michigan he brought together the leadership of the often warring Klans and other white racist groups for well over a decade, assiduously forging links among the different groups and tying together a political overground that has played off a small, but violent, underground. A former Republican Party leader and insurance executive, he became a grand dragon of the Ku Klux Klan in Michigan and headed up George Wallace's 1968 presidential campaign in that state before moving on to forge his own vision of white America's future.

Politician and former Klan leader David Duke has achieved the movement's political high-water mark in his emergence as a third-party candidate in the 1988 presidential election, as a Louisiana State legislator, and, in 1990, as a candidate for the U.S. Senate. He is a product of the Klans' self-transformation in the mid-seventies: a young, handsome, college-educated racist. Before entering party politics, Duke took over a small Klan faction called the Knights of the Ku Klux Klan, based in Louisiana. Under his tutelage, the Klan took on a

American Nazi Party

Aryan Nations supporters join skinheads and Klansmen at a Pulaski, Tennessee rally, October 7, 1989.

new buttoned-down image, advancing the notions of separatism and "equal rights for all races."

Tom Metzger, a television repairman from southern California and the leader of the San Diego – based White Aryan Resistance (WAR), appears to have infused the far right with new blood through the burgeoning skinhead movement. Metzger revamped the fading concept of white revolution after its defeat at the hands of the civil rights movement, and made it relevant to a new era. Skinheads are not people who dress up in sheets or Nazi uniforms at night — in fact, they wear their heavy-workboots-and-shaved-head uniforms all day long. The right wing of the skins are becoming the children of the Klan, and they may already be its future.

"This Is Revolution"

In the 1980s, emboldened by the political ascendance of Ronald Reagan and the New Right, the racist fringe announced itself in an accelerating pattern of violence. The decade began with a clash between Bill Wilkinson's Invisible Empire of the Ku Klux Klan and civil rights marchers in Decatur, Alabama in 1979. Four years later the Aryan Nations splinter group that called itself the Order came up from the underground to set out on a rampage of robberies, shootouts, and murders across the country, culminating with the machine gun killing of Alan Berg, a Denver radio talk show host. As the eighties ended, the 1989 Christmas mail bombings in Alabama and Georgia reflected a backdrop of more than a decade of far-right resurgence that exploited the suffering in the depressed farm belt and elsewhere by villifying Jews and people of color. Between 1980 and 1986 there were nearly 3,000 violent racist incidents, including 138 attempted or successful bombings.

Of course, such spectacular exploits drew heavy federal heat, but the hydralike nature of the movement helped it to flourish anyway. When the FBI finally squashed the Order in a paramilitary-style bust on an island off the Washington State coast in the mid-1980s, the revolutionary right sprang up anew with Glenn Miller's White Patriot Party in North Carolina. Since then, Miller's group, too, has been brought to heel; now their erstwhile leader is a government informer, and his followers have splintered into various Klan and Nazi groups around the South. Still, the movement in the South has survived. In 1987, a revivified white power coalition held a prominent anti–civil rights march in Forsyth County, Georgia, where rightist

White Aryan Resistance

leaders, including David Duke, marched shoulder-to-shoulder with members of different Klans and newly recruited Nazi skinheads.

What recent history has shown is unmistakably this: An organized and, at times, violent, new far-right movement has emerged, and its existence has become impossible to ignore.

"This is revolution," Bob Miles told visitors at his farm in 1986. "Like Johnny Appleseed, we've sowed the seeds. I told the FBI in the presence of my lawyer one time, I said, 'It's too late. We've done the work and you can't reverse it. And out there these seeds we know will grow into apple trees and they'll bear fruit.' "

The
Worldwide
Conspiracy

CHAPTER 1

The Worldwide Conspiracy

"The Jew is not a white man." Laverne sat musing on his Nebraska porch in the July evening. Beyond him lay the family farm, now the subject of a heatedly contested foreclosure proceeding with the local bank. "What's the saying, 'blood in the face?'" asked a visitor. "If you can blush you're not a Jew," Laverne nodded, taking a bite of a Dorito chip.

For Laverne, the hidden truth behind the increasingly ominous daily events of his life had been revealed by reading the Bible and subscribing to the biblical interpretations provided by a Christian Identity minister. The arcane theology of Christian Identity provides the underpinning for much of today's racist doctrine. The ideas behind Christian Identity, which originated in Great Britain during the middle of the nineteenth century, represent the most recent twist to the centuries-old myth that holds that Jews are at the heart of a world conspiracy aimed at undermining civil society.

The "Demon Jew"

The evolution of the myth portraying Jews as a demonic force in world history has been central to the spread of racism in Europe and America during the twentieth century. Its role has been to provide what seems to be a simple, sure-fire interpretation of events by which often chaotic and perplexing change can be explained. Christian Identity adds a theological embellishment to the myth, explaining not only that Jews are part of a grand political conspiracy, but also that they, together with people of color, are not really humans at all.

In *Warrant for Genocide*, Norman Cohn's finely detailed investigation of its history, the myth of a worldwide conspiracy with the demonic Jew at its center has been traced back to the early Middle Ages and to stories of plots by two secret societies to overthrow the established order. In its early form, the myth concerned Christian conspirators. Only much later did Jews become the focal point.

There's still HOPE...

But, little TIME...

THE LAST FULL MEASURE!

To fully appreciate the sweep and durability of this myth, it must be viewed in its entirety.

The myth begins in 1797 with the French cleric Abbé Barruel, who wrote a lengthy history on the rise of the revolutionary Jacobins, attempting to explain the causes of the French Revolution. Barruel argued that the Revolution was the result of a conspiracy hatched by the Order of Templars. Founded during the Crusades to protect religious pilgrims in the Holy Land, the secret order had gained great land holdings and financial power in Europe during the Middle Ages, posing a threat to established order until it was crushed and its leaders burned at the stake in 1314. Barruel insisted that the Templars were not really destroyed but continued on through the centuries, working toward the destruction of all monarchies, the overthrow of the Papacy, and the establishment of universal civil liberties for all.

According to Barruel, the Templars had captured control of another secret revolutionary group: the Order of Freemasons, an organization espousing liberal and democratic principles which grew up among the stone masons and cathedral workers during the Middle Ages. And yet another group, Barruel said, was involved in the grand conspiracy that culminated in the French Revolution: It was the Illuminati, established in 1776 by Adam Weishaupt, a Bavarian law professor. Members of this secret society were initiated in progressive stages, achieving "illumination" through the study of rationalistic philosophy and the humanities. Initiates first made confessions of their life histories, and then took oaths of absolute secrecy. Over time, the Illuminati spread through Germany and into France by infiltrating the lodges of Freemasons. However, dissident members eventually revealed the inner workings of the sect to authorities, and it was condemned by the Roman Catholic church and finally dissolved by the Bavarian government in 1786. To some historians, the Illuminati amounted to a rationalistic movement of the Enlightenment. But others portrayed Weishaupt as a hellish fiend, aiming to abolish all authority, and thereby rediscovering and promoting liberty and equality — those basic, primitive human qualities that had been submerged by law and private property. (The Illuminati surfaced in Germany once more at the end of the nineteenth century, then was abolished, along with other secret societies, by Hitler.)

By the end of the eighteenth century, Barruel claimed, the Templars had also organized a secret literary academy whose membership came to include Voltaire, Condorcet, and Diderot. Its writings contributed to the breakdown of public morals and religion among the French, and its adherents went on to build a vast organization that came to be known as the Jacobins, and was instrumental in overthrowing the monarchy of France. Barruel wrote that unless the conspiracy was stopped, it would grow until it ruled the world.

As Cohn notes, Jews did not play any great part in the French Revolution — any more than they helped lay its philosophic foundations — and hence did not figure into Barruel's initial worldwide conspiracy theory. They first became entangled in the myth of conspiracy in 1806, when Barruel received a letter from J.B. Simonini, a retired army officer living in Florence. Simonini applauded Barruel for revealing the "hellish sects which are preparing the way for the Antichrist," and called his attention to the "Judaic sect," which was "the most formidable power, if one considers its great wealth and the protection it enjoys in almost all European countries." Simonini went on to tell how he stumbled onto this great conspiracy at a gathering of Piedmontese Jews in northern Italy. Pretending to be Jewish himself, Simonini

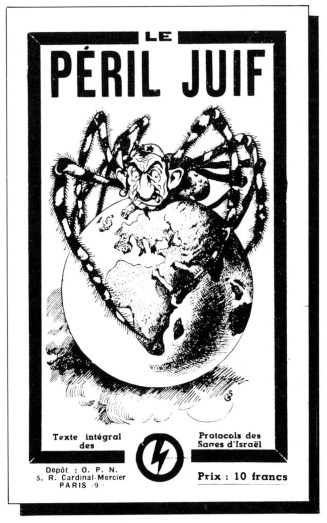

Title page of a 1945 French edition of the Protocols of the Elders of Zion.

said, he eavesdropped on their conversation, learning their innermost secrets. They confided to him that Jews had not only founded the Freemasons and the Illuminati, they had even disguised themselves as Christians and become clergymen, including cardinals and bishops. Soon they hoped to

Protocols
of the Meetings of the Learned Elders of Zion

[In the late nineteenth century various forms of a myth outlining a Jewish conspiracy for world domination began appearing. The following are excerpts of what became known as the Protocols of the Elders of Zion.]

Protocol No. 1

Right lies in Might. Freedom—an idea only . . . It must be noted that men with bad instincts are more in number than the good, and therefore the best results in governing them are attained by violence and terrorization, and not by academic discussions. Every man aims at power, everyone would like to become a dictator if only he could, and rare indeed are the men who would not be willing to sacrifice the welfare of all for the sake of securing their own welfare.

What has restrained the beasts of prey who are called men? What has served for their guidance hitherto?

In the beginnings of the structure of society they were subjected to brutal and blind force; afterwards—to Law, which is the same force, only disguised. I draw the conclusion that by the law of nature right lies in force.

Political freedom is an idea but not a fact. This idea one must know how to apply whenever it appears necessary with this bait of an idea to attract the masses of the people to one's party for the purpose of crushing another who is in authority. This task is rendered easier if the opponent has himself been infected with the idea of freedom, *so-called liberalism*, and, for the sake of an idea, is willing to yield some of his power. It is precisely here that the triumph of our theory appears: the slackened reins of government are immediately, by the law of life, caught up and gathered together by a new hand, because the blind might of the nation cannot for one single day exist without guidance, and the new authority merely fits into the place of the old already weakened by liberalism. . . .

Protocol No. 2

Economic Wars . . . It is indispensable for our purpose that wars, so far as possible, should not result in territorial gains: war will thus be brought on to the economic ground, where the nations will not fail to perceive in the assistance we give the strength of our predominance, and this state of things will put both sides at the mercy of our international *agentur*; which possesses millions of eyes ever on the watch and unhampered by any limitations whatsoever. Our international rights will then wipe out national rights, in the proper sense of right, and will rule the nations precisely as the civil law of States rules the relations of their subjects among themselves. . . .

Protocol No. 4

Stages of a Republic . . . Every republic passes through several stages. The first of these is comprised in the early days of mad raging by the blind mob, tossed hither and thither, right and left: the second is demogogy, from which is born anarchy, and that leads inevitably to despotism—not any longer legal and overt, and therefore responsible despotism, but to unseen and secretly hidden, yet nevertheless sensibly felt despotism in the hands of some secret organization or other, whose acts are the more unscrupulous inasmuch as it works behind a screen, behind the backs of all sorts of agents, the changing of whom not only does not injuriously affect but actually aids the secret force by saving it, thanks to continual changes, from the necessity of expending its resources on the rewarding of long services.

Who and what is in a position to overthrow an invisible force? And this is precisely what our force is. *Gentile* masonry blindly serves as a screen for us and our objects, but the plan of action of our force, even its very abiding-place, remains for the whole people an unknown mystery. . . .

In order to give the *goyim* no time to think and take note, their minds must be diverted towards industry and trade. Thus, all the nations will be swallowed up in the pursuit of gain and in the race for it will not take note of their common foe. But again, in order that freedom may once for all disintegrate and ruin the communities of the *goyim*, we must put industry on a speculative basis: the result of this will be that what is withdrawn from the land by industry will slip through the hands and pass into speculation, that is, to our classes. . . .

Protocol No. 5

Creation of an intensified centralization of government . . . What form of administrative rule can be given to communities in which corruption has penetrated everywhere, communities where riches are attained only by the clever surprise tactics of semi-swindling tricks; where looseness reigns: where morality is maintained by penal measures and harsh laws but not by voluntarily accepted principles: where the feelings toward faith and country are obliterated by cosmopolitan convictions? What form of rule is to be given to these communities if not that despotism which I shall describe to you later? We shall create an intensified centralization of government in order to grip in our hands all the forces of the community. . . .

Protocol No. 6

Monopolies . . . We shall soon begin to establish huge monopolies, reservoirs of colossal riches, upon which even large fortunes of the *goyim* will depend to such an extent that they will go to the bottom together with the credit of the States on the day after the political smash. . . .

At the same time we must intensively patronize trade and industry, but, first and foremost, speculation, the part played by which is to provide a counterpoise to industry: the absence of speculative industry will multiply capital in private hands and will serve to restore agriculture by freeing the land from indebtedness to the land banks. What we want is that industry should drain off from the land both labour and capital and by means of speculation transfer into our hands all the money of the world, and thereby throw all the *goyim* into the ranks of the proletariat. Then the *goyim* will bow down before us, if for no other reason but to get the right to exist.

To complete the ruin of the industry of the *goyim* we shall bring to the assistance of speculation the luxury which we have developed among the *goyim*, that greedy demand for luxury which is swallowing up everything. *We shall raise the rate of wages which, however, will not bring any advantage to the workers, for at the same time, we shall produce a rise in prices of the first necessaries of life, alleging that it arises from the decline of agriculture and cattle-breeding: we shall further undermine artfully and deeply sources of production, by accustoming the workers to anarchy and to drunkenness and side by side therewith taking all measure to extirpate from the fact of the earth all the educated forces of the* GOYIM.

In order that the true meaning of things may not strike the GOYIM *before the proper time we shall mask it under an alleged ardent desire to serve the working classes and the great principles of political economy about which our economic theories are carrying on an energetic propaganda.* . . .

have a Jew named Pope. Unwitting Christians had already granted these impostors full civil rights, allowing them to buy up land and houses to such an extent that true Christians would be dispossessed, their churches made over into synagogues, and they themselves reduced to slaves.

As time went on, Cohn explains, the myth of the "demon Jew" received further embellishment. Seventy-five years after Simonini's revelations, *Biarritz*, a novel by Sir John Retcliffe (a pen name for Hermann Goedsche, an official in the Prussian postal service), gained great popularity across Europe. It contained a spooky chapter entitled "In the Jewish Cemetery in Prague," which described how once every hundred years, the reigning elders of the twelve tribes of Israel gathered around the grave of the most senior rabbi and issued reports on the progress of the grand plot to enslave the gentiles and take over the world.

This story of the Prague cemetery was published in pamphlet form throughout Russia and then in France. At first it was treated as fiction, then gradually, through repetition, it became accepted as fact. Over time the form of the diatribe changed, and the different speeches were consolidated into one speech by the head rabbi, made before a secret meeting of Jews. It became known as "The Rabbi's Speech," and it was published as such across Europe.

These different versions of the Jewish conspiracy myth, printed over the course of the nineteenth century, provided the basic plot line of the notorious *Protocols of the Elders of Zion*. Again, in the case of the *Protocols*, a fantastic fiction soon became widely accepted as fact. The *Protocols* are framed by a fantasy in which a world congress of leading Jews has gathered in Cracow, Poland in 1840 to plot the best means for spreading Judaism across the globe. The book itself consists of a series of written lectures in which a member of the purported secret Jewish government — the Elders of Zion — lays out a plot for world domination. There are twenty-four chapters, about 1,200 pages in all.

In brief, the *Protocols* argue that people are incapable of governing themselves, and only a despot using armed force can rule effectively. For years, the *Protocols* say, the Jews have plotted this course, and now they must rise to power by pitting the gentiles against one another until, eventually, the Jews will be able to enlist the masses in overthrowing their indolent gentile leaders. Thereafter the masses will be kept under firm control through an efficient government that will banish unemployment, apply taxation in proportion to wealth, encourage small business, and promote education. During this messianic age the Jewish masters will shrewdly promise, but never deliver, liberty.

The *Protocols* appeared in Russia at the turn of the century, where they helped to whip up the emotion behind the pogroms. Later, they were the subject of articles, reviews, and editorials by the *Times* and the *Spectator* in England, and they were eagerly embraced in Germany, where the German defeat in World War I was widely blamed on a Jewish conspiracy. A correspondent for the London *Times* then discovered that, in part, the *Protocols* were a plagiarism, copied from an 1865 pamphlet attacking Napoleon III, written by Maurice Joly and entitled *Dialogue aux Enfers entre Montesquieu et Machiavel*. And it was revealed that a later version of the *Protocols* had probably been concocted on instructions from the head of the Czar's secret police shortly before the Russian Revolution, as part of an intrigue against revolutionaries living outside Russia. These bogus *Protocols* nevertheless became the version of the myth that has lasted to this day, the greatest continuing fabrication in history to withstand the scrutiny of an age of supposedly rational thought.

Birth of a Nation

The story of the worldwide Jewish conspiracy would eventually make its way across the Atlantic, where it would find a sympathetic audience in America amidst the anti-alien atmosphere of the 1920s.

Drawing of Ku Klux Klansmen which appeared in an 1868 issue of Harper's *magazine.*

LIBRARY OF CONGRESS

More than seventy-five years after the French Revolution, the United States was struggling to recover from the aftermath of the Civil War. In Pulaski, Tennessee in 1866, half a dozen recently returned — and bored — Confederate soldiers who were looking around for a source of amusement formed an organization they called the Ku Klux Klan. Members would turn up at town gatherings dressed in outlandish outfits and publicly haze their newest recruits. They put together a group for playing practical jokes, like draping themselves in sheets and wandering about town, spooking the public. These early Kluxers had no political consciousness at all; their only stated purpose was "to have fun, make mischief, and play pranks on the public." But soon they turned to newly freed blacks as a source of humor, recounting stories of how their nighttime hijinks frightened the freedmen.

As its reputation for merry pranks grew, the Klan took on the trappings of a full-fledged civic organization. One of the founders, George Gordon, imposed a military-style hierarchy. Subsequently, its organizational structure borrowed heavily both from the secret societies that made up the anti-immigrant Know-Nothing movement and from the Knights of the Golden Circle, another band of ex–Confederate soldiers who had come up with the idea of conquering Mexico and the northern part of South America to provide space for new slave states.

Within a few months of its appearance, Nathan Bedford Forrest, a former slave trader and distinguished Confederate general, became head of the Klan, and provided it with a semblance of real organization. Before the election of 1868 the Klan became overtly political, arrayed against northern carpetbaggers. It began to purposefully intimidate blacks and their white northern teachers in nighttime raids. By the spring of that year, the Klan in

Tennessee had become a vigilante army. In anticipation of the year's election they began to terrorize blacks, whipping them and breaking up voting efforts. Forrest claimed there were 40,000 Klansmen in Tennessee alone, and some 550,000 across the South. But as the Klan spread, any form of central control was lost. Forrest wanted out and issued an order for the Klan to disband — which went unheeded.

Klan terror actually grew worse as its superstructure broke down. After several attempts to control the Klan, Congress made night riding a crime, gave the president the authority to use troops to put down civil disturbances, and, for a limited period of time, suspend habeas corpus. In 1871, President Ulysses S. Grant ordered troops to march back from the Indian wars on the western plains to help South Carolina's governor put down Klan violence. A military investigation led to mass arrests, and the Klan dissolved.

Grant's move against the revanchist Confederates ended the Klan as a united organization, but it could not really end the "idea" of the Klan. For much of American history, the Ku Klux Klan has been a refrain that never quite fades away, a periodically renewable siren call of white supremacy.

After the First World War, the Klan rose once again — this time appealing to a far wider spectrum of the population. By the mid-1920s its membership amounted to three or four million. In part, its appeal lay in a nativist reaction against rapid and unsettling change, in a nostalgia for a simpler time. Its popularity increased as the result of an alliance with Protestant fundamentalism, itself undergoing a resurgence in the face of theological challenge. And the Klan gained great notoriety with the release in 1915 of D. W. Griffith's film *Birth of a Nation*. While the film represented a great cinematic innovation, its content amounted to a romantic whitewash of the Klan's history: It had been based on *The Clansman* by Thomas Dixon, Jr., a syrupy novel of the Klan during radical reconstruction.

In those days the imperial wizard — the head of the Klan — was William Joseph (Doc) Simmons. Simmons was a former minister, and he had modelled Klan ceremonies on church ritual. Klan leaders set out to attract the clergy, appealing to nativist intolerance, fundamentalist frustration with the libertinism of the Roaring Twenties, and the general anti-modernist urge of the heartland.

THE CLANSMAN

"'Do you not fear my betrayal of your secret?'"

The Clansman
An Historical Romance of the Ku Klux Klan

[Thomas Dixon, Jr.'s 1905 novel about the Klan following the Civil War inspired D.W. Griffith's innovative and enormously popular 1915 film Birth of a Nation. *What follows are excerpts from the book.]*

. . . As the crowds returned to their homes, no notice was taken of a dozen men on horseback who rode out of town by different ways about dusk. At eight o'clock they met in the woods, near the first little flag-station located on McAllister's farm four miles from Piedmont, where a buggy awaited them. Two men of powerful build, who were strangers in the county, alighted from the buggy and walked along the track to board the train at the station three miles beyond and confer with the conductor.

The men, who gathered in the woods, dismounted, removed their saddles, and from the folds of the blankets took a white disguise for horse and man. In a moment it was fitted on each horse, with buckles at the throat, breast, and tail, and the saddles replaced. The white robe for the man was made in the form of an ulster overcoat with cape, the skirt extending to the top of the shoes. From the red belt at the waist were swung two revolvers which had been concealed in their pockets. On each man's breast was a scarlet circle within which shone a white cross. The same scarlet circle and cross appeared on the horse's breast, while on his flanks flamed the three red mystic letters, K. K. K. Each man wore a white cap, from the edges of which fell a piece of cloth extending to the shoulders. Beneath the visor was an opening for the eyes and lower down one for the mouth. On the front of the caps of two of the men appeared the red wings of a hawk as the ensign of rank. . . .

At the signal of a whistle, the men and horses arrayed in white and scarlet swung into double-file cavalry formation and stood awaiting orders. The moon was now shining brightly, and its light shimmering on the silent horses and men with their tall spiked caps made a picture such as the world had not seen since the Knights of the Middle Ages rode on their Holy Crusades.

As the train neared the flag-station, which was dark and unattended, the conductor approached Gus, leaned over, and said: "I've just gotten a message from the sheriff telling me to warn you to get off at this station and slip into town. There's a crowd at the depot there waiting for you and they mean trouble."

Gus trembled, and whispered: "Den fur Gawd's sake lemme off here."

The two men who got on at the station below stepped out before the negro, and, as he alighted from the car, seized, tripped, and threw him to the ground. The engineer blew a sharp signal, and the train pulled on. In a minute Gus was bound and gagged.

One of the men drew a whistle and blew twice. A single tremulous call like the cry of an owl answered. The swift beat of horses' feet followed, and four white-and-scarlet clansmen swept in a circle around the group.

One of the strangers turned to the horseman with red-winged ensign on his cap, saluted, and said: "Here's your man, Night Hawk." . . .

The clansmen blindfolded the negro, placed him on a horse, tied his legs securely, and his arms behind him to the ring in the saddle.

The Night Hawk blew his whistle four sharp blasts, and his pickets galloped from their positions and joined him. Again the signal rang, and his men wheeled with the precision of trained cavalrymen into column formation three abreast, and rode toward Piedmont, the single black figure tied and gagged in the centre of the white-and-scarlet squadron.

As a crowd looks on, William Brown is burned to death in 1919 in Omaha, Nebraska — one of many murders of black men by whites in the years following World War I.

Klan leaders descended on local fundamentalist ministers, sympathizing with them over rising crime rates and the pernicious evils of bootlegging, promising to help them increase church attendance by arguing that the Klan was the one force equipped to deal with the deterioration of society. Klan propaganda stressed the joining of Christ and the Klan: "We honor the Christ as the Klansman's Only *Criterion of Character*. And we seek at His hands that cleansing from sin and impurity which only He can give." As Wyn Craig Wade notes in his book *The Fiery Cross*:

Possibly as many as 40,000 ministers joined the Klan. Many of them became the first Exalted Cyclopes of their local communities. In Pennsylvania, Texas, North Dakota, and Colorado, they became Grand Dragons of their entire states. Others preached pro-Klan sermons from their pulpits, turned their churches over to Klan meetings, spoke at Klan rallies, or became national lecturers for Imperial Headquarters. (Of the thirty-nine Klokards, or national lecturers, employed by the Klan, twenty-six were fundamentalist ministers.) In Missouri, Iowa, Indiana, Ohio, North Carolina, New Jersey, Rhode Island, and Maine the support of the clergy was indispensable to Klan growth.

Even rank-and-file ministers of the Mormon Church of Jesus Christ of Latter-day Saints joined the Klan.

Ministers who joined were bombarded with Klan publications. (The Klan owned or controlled 150 different magazines.) As Wade tells the story, the high point of a clerical induction was a "church visitation," when suddenly, during a long, snoozy sermon, the church doors would swing open and down the aisle would march a group of hooded Klansmen. The service, naturally, would halt abruptly, and a Klansman would make a speech that ended with him handing the minister a note, often accompanied by a contribution. "Dear Mr. Jeeter," began the note handed to the Reverend Jerry Jeeter in Phoenix, "The Unseen, All Seeing Eye has looked upon you and the noble work you are doing and found it good. We know that you stand for Law, Order, Decency and Christianity. . . . We, like you, fear none but God, whose work you are doing."

The Klan's campaign to recruit fundamentalist ministers was celebrated as "the return of the Puritans in this corrupt and jazz-mad age." Bootlegging was a particular target, and while the Klan viewed Jews as "insoluble and indigestible," they really hit a resonant chord of response by reviving what might at first have seemed to be a tired theme: Pope bashing. Catholicism, as one minister described it, was nothing more than "Christianity in an Italian dress." The KKK played on this theme so successfully that by 1925 it had more members than ever, and played a vociferous role in the smear campaign aimed at Al Smith, the Roman Catholic Democratic presidential candidate in 1928. The height of the Klan's political success occurred with the passage, in 1924, of a bill which placed strict quotas on immigration, strongly favoring white Anglo-Saxon Protestants.

But the rise of the Klan brought on a backlash. Newspapers began to print lengthy exposés of Klan terror, and one state after another passed "anti-masking" laws aimed at the hooded terrorists. Such disparate groups as the American Federation of Labor and the American Legion came out against the Klan. People were outraged at the murder of a young white woman, Marge Oberholzer, in Indiana by one of the nation's most powerful Klan leaders, David Curtis Stephenson. Upon his conviction, Stephenson turned against the Klan and, from his jail cell, told all about the group's operations, including election graft. Other events also worked against the Klan. In 1925 the "Scopes Monkey Trial"—in which a Tennessee public school teacher was tried for teaching Darwinism—turned public opinion against the Klan's allies in the fundamentalist churches. Just as quickly as it had risen at the start of the decade, the Klan withered away. In the mid-1920s it had boasted a membership of four million. By the decade's end that number had dwindled to 40,000.

Fordism

It was during the height of the Klan's popularity and its embrace of Protestant fundamentalism during the 1920s that the myth of the worldwide Jewish conspiracy took root in the United States. Henry Ford, the automobile tycoon, became the myth's main publicist.

In 1920s America, the uncertainties and rapid change of the Jazz Age hastened the spread of narrow-minded, puritanical Protestantism, encouraged anti-Papist prejudice, and sent thousands of people to thumbing their Bibles for the earliest sign of a Second Coming. The era also provided a receptive atmosphere for an equally encompassing secular myth: the myth of the centuries-old plot by Jews to capture control of the world. At the

Ku Klux Klan parade in Washington, D.C. in 1925.

same time that discomfited Protestant preachers were providing the seedbed for a rapid expansion of the Klan, the new and burgeoning auto industry of Henry Ford was financing the spread of the theory of an insidious Jewish conspiracy, and Ford was becoming the most enthusiastic and successful booster of the *Protocols of the Elders of Zion*. Ford's Michigan newspaper, the weekly *Dearborn Independent*, became an outspoken and effective popularizer of the myth of the international Jewish plot.

As historian Leo P. Ribuffo explains in his article "Henry Ford and *The International Jew*," Ford's involvement apparently began sometime before the summer of 1920, when one of his representatives met a Russian émigré, Paquita de Shishmareff, who claimed to know all about Jewish operations in Europe. She passed along a copy of the *Protocols*, which was studied by the *Dearborn Independent*'s staff. In July the paper began to publish a series of articles on the "International Jew," which were based on the supposed international conspiracy as set forth in the *Protocols*. After the articles appeared, Ford and his associates widened their dealings with Russian royalists loyal to the Czar. One of Ford's representatives in Paris even obtained a report by a former Russian judge purporting to show that Jewish conspirators had murdered the ruling family, the Romanovs.

Transplanted from Europe to an American setting, the *Protocols* took on an entirely new luster. In Russia, Norman Cohn argues in *Warrant for Genocide*, the *Protocols* reflected the twisted minds of right-wingers, who put into the mouths of Jews their own thoughts, fears, and insecurities. Similarly, Ribuffo notes, in America, Henry Ford's staff used the worldwide Jewish conspiracy to explain the unsettling social changes underway since the Civil War. The *Dearborn Independent* complained that the rise of monopolies and spread of big government produced a "steady curtailment" of freedom. The tendency towards systematization, the rise of "public health" and "public safety," made people even more bound to the state. The *Independent* worried about the decline in family values, and questioned the "endless stream" of immigrants who were reducing New York City to chaos. The paper was concerned with determining "truth" in the increasingly confusing modern world: Whether or not the *Protocols* were accurate, they provided a working interpretation of what was going on.

According to the *Independent*'s analysis, Jews used ideas to "corrupt Collective Opinion," controlled finance, sponsored revolution, and were "everywhere" exercising power. Over the centuries, it said, Jews had created financial institutions to maximize profits and influence, and to spread radical doctrine — and during the French Revolution, they had come close to victory. As Ribuffo tells it, the thinking was that Jews had predicted the outbreak of World War I and had profited from the conflict. Jewish financier Jacob Schiff had bankrolled Japan's war against Russia in 1905, and had encouraged the Japanese to spread revolutionary propaganda among Russian prisoners of war, helping to bring about the Russian Revolution. After this success in Russia, the Jews turned to Germany.

According to the *Independent*'s analysis, Jews had also played a major role in America from the start: Columbus "consorted much" with them. They inserted their cliquish commercial practices into seventeenth-century New York. During the American Revolution, some Jews consorted with Benedict Arnold, and the Rothschild family arranged the use of Hessian mercenaries by the British forces, earning millions of dollars in profits. Later, Jews gained power over presidents: In 1911, they forced William Howard Taft to break the Russian-American commercial treaty, at great cost to the czarist regime. Jews surrounded Woodrow Wilson from the start of his administration, and gained even more influence after the beginning of World War I. Bernard Baruch, chairman of the War Industries Board, reigned supreme as the "Jewish High Governor of the United States."

The *Independent* also claimed that by the end of the war, Jews had tightened their grip on the American economy. They were money lenders, eschewing any role in production. In 1913 Paul Warberg, a German Jew, "emigrated to the States for the express purpose of changing our financial system," finally convincing Congress to pass the

The International Jew

[The International Jew *was compiled from a series of essays that began appearing in Henry Ford's newspaper, the* Dearborn Independent, *in 1920. The following excerpts reflect the spirit of this influential book.*]

Theater and Cinema

The Theater has long been a part of the Jewish program for the guidance of public taste and the influencing of the public mind. Not only is the theater given a special place in the program of the Protocols, but it is the instant ally night by night and week by week of any idea which the "power behind the scenes" wishes to put forth. . . .

Not only the "legitimate" stage, so-called, but the motion picture industry—the fifth greatest of all industries—is also entirely Jew-controlled. . . .

Every night hundreds of thousands of people give from two to three dollars to the Theater, every day literally millions of people give up from 30 minutes to 3 hours to the "Movies"; and this simply means that millions of Americans every day place themselves voluntarily within range of Jewish ideas of life, love and labor; within close range of Jewish propaganda, sometimes cleverly, sometimes clumsily concealed. This gives the Jewish masseur of the public mind all the opportunity he desires; and his only protest now is that exposure may make his game a trifle difficult. . . .

The screen, whether consciously or just carelessly, is serving as a rehearsal stage for scenes of anti-social menace. There are no uprisings of revolutions except those that are planned and rehearsed. Revolutions are not spontaneous uprisings, but carefully planned minority actions. There have been few popular revolutions. Civilization and liberty have always been set back by those revolutions which subversive elements have succeeded in starting. Successful revolution must have a rehearsal. It can be done better in the motion pictures than anywhere else: this is the "visual education" such as even the lowest brow can understand. Indeed, there is a distinct disadvantage in being "high-brow" in such matters. Normal people shake their heads and pucker their brows and wring their hands, saying, "We cannot understand it." Of course, they cannot. But if they understood the low-brow, they would understand it, and very clearly. There are two families in this world, and on one the darkness dwells. . . .

Popular Music

Many people have wondered whence come the waves upon waves of musical slush that invade decent homes and set the young people of this generation imitating the drivel of morons. *Popular music is a Jewish monopoly.* Jazz is a Jewish creation. The mush, slush, the sly suggestion, the abandoned sensuousness of sliding notes, are of Jewish origin.

Monkey talk, jungle squeals, grunts and squeaks and gasps suggestive of calf love are camouflaged by a few feverish notes and admitted in homes where the thing itself, unaided by "canned music," would be stamped out in horror. The fluttering music sheets disclose expressions taken directly from the cesspools of modern capitals, to be made the daily slang, the thoughtlessly hummed remarks of school boys and girls.

Is it surprising that whichever way you turn to trace the harmful streams of influence that flow through society, you come upon a group of Jews? In baseball corruption—a group of Jews. In exploitative finance—a group of Jews. In theatrical degeneracy—a group of Jews. In liquor propaganda—a group of Jews. In control of national war policies—a group of Jews. In control of the Press through business and financial pressure—a group of Jews. War profiteers, 80 per cent of them—Jews. Organizers of active opposition to Christian laws and customs—Jews. . . .

The "song-pluggers" of theater, vaudeville and radio, are the paid agents of the Yiddish song agencies. Money, and not merit, dominates the spread of the moron music which is styled Jewish jazz and swing. Non-Jewish music is stigmatized as "high-brow." The people are fed from day to day on the moron suggestiveness that flows in a slimy flood out of "Tin-Pan-Alley," the head factory of filth in New York which is populated by the "Abies," the "Izzies," and the "Moes" who make up the composing staffs of the various institutions . . . Flocks of young girls who thought they could sing, and others who thought they could write song poems, came to the neighborhood allured by the dishonest advertisements that promised more than the budding Yiddish promoters could fulfill. Needless to say, scandal became rampant, as it always does when so-called "Gentile" girls are reduced to the necessity of seeking favors from the Jew. It was the constant shouting of voices, the hilarity of "parties," the banging of pianos and the blaring of trombones that gave the district the name of "Tin-Pan-Alley." All America is now one great Tin-Pan-Alley, its entertainment, its youth, its politics, a blare of moronic Judaism. . . .

Liquor

The claim made for the Jews that they are a sober race may be true, but that has not obscured two facts concerning them; namely, that they usually constitute the liquor dealers of countries where they live in numbers, and that in the United States they were the only race exempted from the operations of the Prohibition Law. In general, the Jews are on the side of liquor and always have been. . . .

Baseball

Whether baseball as a first-class sport is killed and will survive only as a cheap-jack entertainment; or whether baseball possesses sufficient intrinsic character to rise in righteous wrath and cast out the danger that menaces it, will remain a matter of various opinion. But there is one certainty, namely, that the last and most dangerous blow dealt baseball was curiously notable for its Jewish character. . . .

To begin with, the Jews are not sportsmen. This is not set down in complaint against them, but merely as analysis. It may be a defect in their character, or it may not; it is nevertheless a fact which discriminating Jews unhesitatingly acknowledge. Whether this is due to their physical lethargy, their dislike of unnecessary physical action, or their cast of mind, others may decide; the Jew is not naturally an out-of-door sportsman; if he takes up golf it is because his station in society calls for it, not that he really likes it; and if he goes in for collegiate athletics, as some of the younger Jews are doing, it is because so much attention has been called to their neglect of sports that the younger generation thinks it necessary to remove that occasion of remark. . . .

Wrestling

Wrestling is so tightly controlled by Jewish managers that a real wrestler is absolutely barred out, for fear he will be able to show that the handful of wrestlers hired by the Jewish Sports Trust are not wrestlers at all, but only impositions on the good nature of the public. The rottenness of the ancient sport of clean wrestling has surfaced in such disgusting orgies as "all in" and "mud" wrestling and, lately, wrestling contests between screaming viragos of the female sex. Wrestling is as much a Jewish *business* controlled in its every part as the manufacture of clothing. . . .

Federal Reserve Act. The Federal Reserve Board aided the "banking aristocracy" in centralizing the economy and increasing funds for speculation. Soon, said the *Independent*, New York was being run by a Jewish community group through gentile fronts. A path was being paved for the first Jewish presi-dent — probably Supreme Court Justice Louis Brandeis. Communism was a concoction of Jewish investors. The Jews had forced gentiles out of the liquor trust. They dominated the entertainment industry, and they had ruined the theater. While America moved forward through individual initia-

Henry Ford receives the Grand Cross of the German Eagle in 1938 from Fritz Hailer (left), German consul in Detroit, and Karl Kapp, German consul in Cleveland.

tive, Jews took advantage of racial loyalty and solidarity.

During this time, the *Dearborn Independent* was often given away, and was compulsory reading in Ford agencies and dealerships nationwide. Its series of articles on the Jewish conspiracy was eventually repackaged as a book entitled *The International Jew*. Half a million copies of the book were circulated in the United States.

The International Jew was translated into sixteen languages, and became a staple in Nazi propaganda. In his book *Under Cover*, J.R. Carlson noted that Ford was the only American to be favorably mentioned in *Mein Kampf*, and the first American awarded the Grand Cross of the German Eagle. He was reported to have helped finance the National Socialists. When Hitler heard Ford might run for president in 1923, he said, according to a *Chicago Tribune* dispatch, "I wish I could send some of my shock troops to Chicago and other big American cities to help in the elections. . . . We look to Heinrich Ford as the leader of the growing fascist movement in America. . . . We have just had his anti-Jewish articles translated and published. The book is being circulated in millions throughout Germany." As Norman Cohn concludes, "All in all *The International Jew* probably did more than any other work to make the *Protocols* world-famous."

Publication of *The International Jew* raised a storm of protest in the United States, with President Wilson himself at its head. In 1927, Ford denied responsibility for the newspaper articles and the book. He claimed he never knew about their publication, and had been deceived by trusted associates. He then retracted the accusations in *The International Jew*, sought to take the book out of circulation, and closed down the *Dearborn Independent*. But since Ford owned both publications,

and had sent his private detectives into New York to get to the bottom of the "secret government," his statements were clearly self-serving. *The International Jew* continued to be sold: In the 1980s it could still be found on sale, along with the *Protocols*, at right-wing gatherings in the Midwest, and was still listed in book catalogues offered by far-right organizations.

Henry Ford did much to spread the myth of the world Jewish conspiracy in the 1920s. It also found easy acceptance, and was propelled forward on the nativist currents of the time. The myth provided a "hidden history" that could explain economic bad times, as well as the turmoil caused by the rapid change from a rural to an urban-dwelling nation. In addition, it served the purposes of Protestant fundamentalists who were looking for signs of the end of the world. By the 1930s the myth was becoming part of a religious revival, and had entered into mainstream politics. Its progress was marked by three important figures, whose stories have been explored by Ribuffo in his illuminating book, *The Old Christian Right*. They were William Dudley Pelley, a sentimental novelist who founded an American version of the Nazi storm troopers called the Silver Shirts; Gerald B. Winrod, a fundamentalist preacher in Kansas who employed the Jewish conspiracy in his own evolving theocratic ideas; and Gerald L.K. Smith, the gifted orator who worked for populist Louisiana governor and senator Huey Long, and who then tried to carry on Long's political machine after his assassination. Smith carried the idea of the Jewish conspiracy with him as he meddled in right-wing politics up until his death in the late 1970s.

The Most Dangerous Man in America

Of the three men who helped to spread the "demon Jew" myth in mid–twentieth century America, William Dudley Pelley came to play the most ironic role. He started out as a novelist, discovered Hitler in a personal mystical experience, and in the end became famous after Franklin Roosevelt, anxious to quash his enemies on the right, seized Pelley and other rightists and charged them with sedition.

As a young man, Pelley worked in his father's New England toilet paper factory. When that failed, he wrote for newspapers (including the *Boston Globe*), and even owned two small country papers.

When these collapsed, he turned to writing short stories for magazines, and by the early 1920s had published more than two hundred stories in *Redbook*, *Collier's*, and the *Saturday Evening Post*. He journeyed to Japan and, after the Russian Revolution broke out, he served with a YMCA canteen in Siberia and wrote dispatches for the Associated Press.

As Ribuffo explains in *The Old Christian Right*, at this stage Pelley admired Woodrow Wilson and supported the League of Nations. At the same time, he was appalled by the Soviets, and warned that the rise of the Industrial Workers of the World signalled an outbreak of American bolshevism.

In 1927, after writing several romantic novels and numerous movie scripts, Pelley withdrew to the mountains of California and underwent a mystical religious rebirth that changed his life: He claimed to have made contact with the occult, hearing voices from other worlds. Pelley soon began to publish an occultist journal called *Liberation*, in which he told how a "Great Time of Troubles" would correct humanity's weaknesses. He believed Christ would return during his lifetime, and reported various sightings.

Pelley discovered that many "demon" souls had been reincarnated — including, for example, one who had resided in Genghis Khan and was then living in Joseph Stalin. By 1931 he decided that the worst demon souls lived in Jewish bodies, through which they were wreaking havoc on the nation. President Herbert Hoover, he said, was being controlled by agents of the "international Shylock" — the Jewish bankers who had engineered the Great Depression.

When Hitler became chancellor of Germany in 1933, Pelley announced the formation of the Silver Legion, better known as the Silver Shirts,

Silver Shirts leader William Pelley, shown here as he appeared before Congress in 1940.

modelled after Hitler's Brown Shirts. The Silver Shirts' express purpose was to bring the "work of Christ militant into the open." The way Pelley saw it, the creation of the Silver Shirts amounted to a "sociological application" of what he had written in *Liberation* — it was an embryonic movement towards a new theocratic state. He proclaimed

Christ an honorary Silver Shirt, and said that Jesus had accepted the commission.

With Pelley as their "Chief," the Silver Shirts openly supported Hitler, cooperated with the pro-Nazi German-American Bund, and embarked on a program of vicious anti-Semitism. By 1940, Pelley claimed, there were 25,000 members of the Silver

Shirts, and 75,000 sympathizers. A more plausible estimate was 400 to 800 members when the legion was launched in 1933, growing to a peak of perhaps 15,000 the following year — only to decline to around 5,000 by 1938. Most of the Silver Shirts' activity was concentrated in a few places: Minneapolis, San Diego, Los Angeles, Seattle, Chicago, and the industrial areas around Cleveland. Members comprised both the working and middle classes.

In 1942 President Roosevelt charged Pelley and others with violation of the Espionage Act for distributing information aimed at subversion of the U.S. armed forces. While the ensuing prosecution was ludicrous in the extreme — making Pelley appear to be far more important than he was — the defense was weak, and the jury convicted him on all counts. Pelley was sentenced to fifteen years in prison, becoming, thanks to the Roosevelt administration, a political martyr.

The Prairie School

Meanwhile, out on the plains of Kansas, another American prefiguration of fascism took form around Gerald B. Winrod, a Protestant fundamentalist minister who gained a large and militant following across the Midwest. His popular publication, the *Defender*, argued that "Nazism and fascism are patriotic and nationalist."

As Ribuffo explains in *The Old Christian Right*, Winrod, like Pelley, promoted the usual anti-Semitic myths, but unlike the muddled mystic in the mountains of California, Winrod professed that his anti-Semitism was firmly anchored in biblical prophecy. Young Gerald Winrod underwent a conversion at age eleven — after God "cured" his mother of terminal cancer — and began preaching at age twelve. After briefly editing a small newspaper called *Jesus is Coming Soon*, Winrod set off on

the evangelical circuit, seeking souls to save. He soon became a major force in the fundamentalist reaction to modern Protestantism — preaching back-to-the-Bible basics, opposition to the teachings of Darwin, and adherence to the dispensationalist belief that Christ would soon return during the great battle of Armageddon. In 1925, he and a group of like-minded ministers and laymen met in Salina, Kansas to establish the Defenders of the Christian Faith which, together with Winrod's magazine the *Defender*, would carry on the fight against liberal Protestantism.

For Winrod, the history of the Jewish conspiracy was illuminated by the Bible and its prophecies. Winrod claimed he never wished any harm to Jews, the great masses of whom, he said, were unaware of the sordid plot, and he considered the story of the Elders of Zion as symbolic. As Ribuffo notes, Winrod "combined familiar anti-Semitic lore and conservative theology to produce an extraordinarily coherent theory of social subversion by a 'certain element' of world Jewry." In short, he believed that the Bible's two Testaments demonstrated that Jews had always been a rebellious people, whose elite had consolidated their system of political power under Solomon, and had overseen the trial and execution of Jesus, as well as the persecution of early Christians under the Roman Empire. These early elders had also composed the Talmud, the code anticipating the *Protocols*.

Scripture, Winrod would say, is "history written in advance," and he himself further advanced the myth of the international Jewish conspiracy by placing it at the center of a revived Protestant fundamentalism — which, of course, warmly embraced the Ku Klux Klan. And Winrod went further: He not only preached fundamentalism, but also translated it into politics by running for the Senate in Kansas. Garnering thousands of votes in the Republican primary campaign in 1938, he finished third with support coming from Mennonite communities and from the counties in which the Ku Klux Klan had flourished in the 1920s. In 1942 he, too, was charged with sedition, as part of the attempt by the Roosevelt administration to snuff out the nativist right.

A Demagogue Worth Knowing

Among the most important figures on the far right — indeed, the chief link between the fascism of the thirties and the white resistance groups of today — was Gerald L.K. Smith, founder of the

Gerald L.K. Smith (left) and Bernard A. Doman in 1942, looking over the first issue of The Cross and the Flag.

Christian Nationalist Crusade. Smith grew up in Wisconsin, where he became a minister of the fundamentalist First Christian Church at the age of eighteen. In 1933 he was among the first to join Pelley's Silver Shirts and, in one early letter, Smith wrote Pelley to say he was heading toward St. Louis "with a uniformed squad of young men composing what I believe will be the first Silver Shirt storm troop in America."

When he landed a job at the First Christian Church in Shreveport, Louisiana, the theme of his preaching changed from storm-trooping to rural radicalism. Eventually, he left the church to work for populist politician Huey Long, formerly governor of Louisiana and then a U.S. senator. Long hired Smith as national organizer for his "Share Our Wealth" campaign, an elaborate scheme to decentralize and redistribute wealth in America. Under the Share Our Wealth scheme, no one could earn more than $1 million a year, or amass a fortune exceeding $5 million. With the resulting redistributed wealth, Long proposed to guarantee each American household a radio, a car, and two to three thousand dollars in annual family income.

Smith travelled across Louisiana and spoke to over one million people in 1934. It was thrilling stuff. As T. Harry Williams recounts in his biography of Huey Long, Smith would cry: "Let's pull down those huge piles of gold until there shall be a real job. Not a little old sow-belly, black-eyed pea job but a real spending money, beefsteak and gravy, Chevrolet, Ford in the garage, new suit, Thomas Jefferson, Jesus Christ, red, white and blue job for every man!" People came from all over to hear Smith. Sometimes men pulled pistols on him, and at a stop in Georgia, opponents threatened to hang him. H.L. Mencken said Smith was "the greatest rabble-rouser seen on earth since Apostolic times."

Smith worshipped Huey Long; he called him "Superman," and would slip into Long's hotel room when he was sleeping and curl up on the floor at the foot of his bed.

When Long was assassinated in 1935, Smith made an unsuccessful bid for power in Louisiana. He then tried to hammer out a national third party with Father Charles Coughlin and Francis Townsend. Coughlin was a radio priest whose sermons from the Shrine of the Little Flower in Michigan reached millions of listeners every week. Coughlin's answer to the Great Depression was to stimulate inflation, and to create a monetary system based on silver rather than gold. He wanted the government to abolish the Federal Reserve System and establish a national bank. In the early 1930s Coughlin supported Roosevelt, but turned against the president as time went on. He counselled against American involvement in the Second World War, and in his later years became a virulent anti-Semite.

Francis Townsend was an elderly physician who had come up with a plan to use public money to provide pensions to the elderly. His Old Age Revolving Pension Plan called on the government to provide everyone over sixty with a monthly pension of $150. This idea caught on, and clubs of supportive elderly people sprang up around the country; they lobbied Congress on behalf of the plan, but without success.

The result of the collaboration among Smith, Coughlin, and Townsend was the Union Party, which ran William Lemke against FDR in 1936. But Lemke was a lackluster candidate; in the general election he got fewer than a million votes. And the egos of Coughlin and Smith could not coexist for long in any one party.

After 1936, Smith moved to New York and launched the Committee of One Million (actually, there were only nine charter members), dedicated

XTRA

CALL TO ACTION !!

BULLETIN No. 7
FROM: GERALD L. K. SMITH

Word has just reached me that the enemy is spending $50,000 to con-
fuse our people. Pro-Russian movie stars, pink preachers, and left
wing Jews have joined together to try to drown out the voice of
Christian people in Los Angeles. This letter is a call to ACTION! --
CHRISTIAN ACTION! -- PRAYER! -- DOWNRIGHT HARD WORK!

I have inside information to the effect that our enemies have organized two pieces of strategy in an attempt to distract the attention
of the community and prevent you and your Christian brethen from
concentrating on the theme and the messages of our dynamic rally this
Friday night, July 20, at the Shrine Auditorium. The enemy is doing
the following at great expense.

1.   The pro-Commuinist JEWISH VOICE has issued a call to 10,000
     Jews to picket our meeting. (See enclosed photostat, which,
     in my judgement is the most obscene and blasphemous article
     I have ever seen in print.)

2.   The pro-Communist left wing so-called Council for Civic Unity
     (12 of whose leaders are listed in Senator Tenney's 1945 re-
     port on Subversive Activities in California) is promoting a
     smear rally in another auditorium. A special advertising
     agency has been retained. Movie stars are being publicized.
     Earth and hell are being moved to counteract and smother your
     interest in our great rally Friday night.

We dare not relax. I challenge you in the remaining hours before the
meeting to get on the telephone and call from 5 to 50 people, urging
them to meet you at the Shrine. If they do not have admission cards,
you should come early. Contact the literature desk. Get as many
cards as you need (after thoroughly identifying yourself) and then go
out and meet your friends at the entrance. One extra card is en-
closed.

I promise a sensational announcement. This announcement has not been
made before, and when I make it in the Shrine, it will shake California, and it will be news for every newspaper in the Nation.

Come early! Come early! Come early! Early means: as soon after
6:30 p.m. as possible. Don't be afraid to walk up to the literature
desk, identify yourself, and inquire as to whether or not there is
anything you can do to help. This letter is being sent only to
people whom we believe will bring at least 10 people besides themselves. I hope I have not guessed wrong on you.

The pro-Communist Jews who will parade up and down in front of the
Shrine Friday night will try to agitate you. Pay no attention to
them. The place will be alive with police. It is estimated that
it will require 200 to 300 police to patrol the crowd. Hold
your head high. Walk straight ahead, and when you get inside the
auditorium, look around and compare the people on the inside with the
ones on the outside. Then decide who is right.

                                             G. L. K. S.

July 17, 1945
Los Angeles, California

Facsimile of a 1945 Gerald L.K. Smith flyer urging supporters to turn out for one of his public harangues.

to combating the twin evils of the New Deal and communism. He warned that a communist revolution would overtake New York, its proponents blowing up bridges and tunnels and sealing the city off from the rest of the world. In fact, the businessmen who financed Smith's crusade were far less interested in hunting down communists than they were in combating the rising influence of the CIO and breaking up other unions.

Making few inroads in New York, Smith moved to Detroit, where he met his idol, Henry Ford. The details of the relationship between Smith and Ford have always been murky, but in his biography of Smith, *Minister of Hate*, Glen Jeansonne discovered that Ford gave Smith money for radio broadcasts and lent him several investigators who helped compile what Smith called the "Ford Company Red File," a set of cards listing reported communists. The relationship also helped to fuel Smith's belief in a worldwide Jewish conspiracy. Smith had himself long been a rabid anti-Semite: As a young preacher in Louisiana, he had not only written to William Dudley Pelley, promising to send him a storm troop, but had also attempted to make contact with "Herr Hitler" himself, arguing that the Jews had gotten "out of hand." Henry Ford introduced Smith to the finer details of the purported Jewish conspiracy in the form of the *Dearborn Independent*'s "International Jew" series. "The day came," Smith said, "when I embraced the research of Mr. Ford and his associates and became courageous enough and honest enough and informed enough to use the words: 'Communism is Jewish.' "

In the late 1930s, Smith sought the Republican nomination for the U.S. Senate in Michigan. He lost by a two-to-one margin, but only after the mainstream Republican Party poured all its resources into defeating him.

Smith was a strong isolationist during the Second World War, arguing that all troops should be brought home to form a protective shield around the United States. He believed Hitler was misunderstood, and that it was preposterous to suggest that six million Jews had been killed when, in fact, they were walking around the streets of America, where they had been brought to keep Roosevelt in power. For Smith, Roosevelt was a far more frightening figure than Hitler, and later Smith even propounded the theory that Roosevelt had not really died, but was being kept hidden in an insane asylum by the Jews, who one day would return him as "President of the World."

Smith's denunciations of Roosevelt didn't end with the war, nor did his pleas for isolationism and his support for the Germans, whom, he felt, had been wrongly denounced. He revived a plan, originally set forth by Long, Coughlin, and Townsend, which promised a home for every family, a guaranteed annual income, good farm prices, freedom from government bureaucracy, and a bonus for returning veterans.

Smith played at politics with rapt fascination throughout his life, and tried to wedge himself into one presidential campaign after another. In 1940 he supported John Bricker as an isolationist. In 1944 he favored Charles Lindbergh or Douglas MacArthur. In 1948 he promoted Douglas MacArthur on the Republican side, machinating with the Dixiecrats at the same time. In Smith's estimation, Truman's victory was a great victory for the Jews. Truman and his wife Bess, Smith reported, had enrolled in a course on the study of the Talmud, and the president might actually have Jewish blood in him — his middle initial, Smith said, stood for Solomon. Roosevelt, of course, had been a Jew in disguise, his real name being Rosenfeldt. And Smith's research even uncovered the

FDR Still Alive?

[Samples of Gerald L.K. Smith's startling "revelations."]

The Roosevelt Death: A Super Mystery

Until Eleanor Roosevelt explains to the world why the casket, containing the remains of Franklin D. Roosevelt, was not opened to be viewed by the public, the death of her husband, Franklin D. Roosevelt, will remain an unsolved mystery. . . . Every prominent figure who has passed away in modern times has left behind him a responsible group of friends and relatives who have insisted that his body 'lie in state' to be viewed by the public prior to burial. This custom was not only violated by the Roosevelt family and the White House palace guard as pertains to the public, but even in the case of the eldest son, Jimmy, who barely arrived in time to see the casket lowered into the ground at Hyde Park. . . . Lifetime political henchmen of the ambitious four term President were mystified, dumbfounded, chagrined, even openly embarrassed over the way the matter was handled. . . .

It remained, however, for Joe Stalin, close friend of Franklin D. Roosevelt, to lock the door to the mystery with a double lock. . . . Stalin immediately contacted in person the man who was the Ambassador to the United States, Andrei Gromyko. He instructed Gromyko to go personally to the White House, insist that the casket be opened, and report to him definitely whether or not he was convinced that Franklin D. Roosevelt was dead. . . . The white-haired diplomat, who later was to be unsuccessful in an attempt to consummate the Roosevelt plan for world government, walked briskly to the White House and contacted . . . not the widow, not the private secretary, not the children—but Samuel Rosenman, whom the late President frequently referred to as 'Sammy the Rose.' It is an open secret that 'Sammy the Rose' wrote most of FDR's important speeches, especially those referring to our relationships with Germany, our international political strategy, and domestic measures having to do with the establishment of new and unheard of bureaus. The White House vetoed . . . Gromyko—yes, they vetoed Stalin. Why did Stalin want to know? . . . Why did he doubt the widow?, the family?, the newspapers?, the palace guard? . . . Experienced and keen observers in Washington believe to this very day, and all the arguments that might be brought forth cannot remove their conviction, that Stalin still doubts. . . .

Bobby Kennedy and the Beatles

The so-called popularity of Bobby Kennedy is a psychological twist which has yet to be fully diagnosed. I get the impression that he has deliberately groomed his hair in a goofy manner to strike the sex chord impulse stimulated by the disgraceful and scandalous Beetles. When Kennedy appears in public, he is followed by large numbers of teenage girls whose scream tones are very similar to those that cry out into the night when the long-haired Beatles of England appear on the scene. . . .

The big shock came when [the Beatles] were given royal recognition by the Royal Family of England. This brings up a pet theory of mine which may not sound like logic to everyone, so we will classify it as experimental thinking. The Crowned Prince of England, Prince Charles, has a freakish growth of hair. He has no forehead. His hair grows out immediately above his eyebrows. The present fad among many young men means that young men and boys with open brows have trained their hair to hide their brows so that they appear the way Prince Charles is compelled to appear by the nature of his hair. Stranger things have happened in this world than that the Royal Family has aided in the building up of the Beatles in order that the hair appearance of young Charles might not be as conspicuous. . . .

fact that Eisenhower was a "Swedish Jew." In 1952, he still pined for MacArthur, eventually placing his name, pathetically, on his third party Christian Nationalist ticket.

Smith disliked the Kennedys, whom he thought were fake Catholics, whiskey-drinking whoremongers, and puppets of the international Jews. In 1964 he at first supported George Wallace, only to ask him to withdraw in favor of the superior Goldwater — a man who had stood by Joe McCarthy and the John Birch Society, and who had opposed the 1964 Civil Rights Act. When the Democrats nominated Lyndon Johnson at their convention in Atlantic City — which also featured a protest in which an integrated group calling itself the Mississippi Freedom Democratic Party sought to replace the all-white Mississippi delegation — it was too much for Smith. "I saw pimps in command," he said. "I witnessed the glorification of whoremongers . . . mealy-mouthed Southerners behaving like Judas Iscariot on the night of our Lord's betrayal . . . fine self-respecting white citizens of Mississippi kicked out, and the bloc of blacks manipulated from New York and Moscow permitted to sit in their places."

In 1968, Smith was a Wallace elector in Oklahoma, firm in his belief that a third party run by Wallace could rule out an electoral majority and force the election into the House of Representatives. Always ambivalent towards the internationally inclined Nixon, Smith greatly admired Spiro Agnew for his repeated attacks on liberals and the media. As Jeansonne writes, "Smith found the Nixon family 'wholesome' in contrast to the libertine Kennedys, but he was horrified by a photograph of African blacks kissing Pat Nixon while topless dancers entertained the First Couple."

As time wore on, Smith modified his opinions. By 1972, he had accepted both China and the Soviet Union, supported the United Nations, and grudgingly admitted that "although Kissinger is a Jew, he is one of the greatest diplomats that ever lived." But he had no problem picking Nixon over McGovern (the candidate of "perverts, lesbians, women-Lib fakers, demagogues and downright traitors"). During Watergate Smith staunchly backed Nixon, asserting his support even on the day of the president's resignation, when he declared, "My one criticism of Nixon is that he didn't personally supervise the Watergate raid so that it would have been done right." After the resignation of Nixon and the installation of Ford, Smith put out a plaintive call for a Nixon comeback in 1976, saying he couldn't back Ford because he was an incompetent.

Playing across a nativist terrain, Pelley, Winrod, and Smith each took the myth of a world Jewish conspiracy off in new directions. Pelley's personally evocative experiences transformed Hitler into a figure of the occult, and Roosevelt's backlash transformed Pelley into a political martyr; Winrod brought the worldwide conspiracy into the midst of an emotional fundamentalist revival; and Smith helped push it into mainstream politics.

Of the three men, Smith remains the most intriguing. His life spanned much of the century, and his political activity extended from Huey Long through Richard Nixon and up into the Carter years. Unlike the ragtag group of far-right politicians today, Gerald L.K. Smith spoke to immense crowds — larger than those turning out for any of today's mainstream politicians, who do most of their campaigning on television. He was a galvanizing orator, and he somehow managed to finagle his way into mainstream politics at the highest levels. He was a huckster, pumping out the forerunners of today's direct mail fund-raising letters with the gusto of a tabloid journalist.

Smith rode the cross-currents of nativism, populism, and nationalism, and his influence still lingers in today's far right. Smith's supporters, notably Wesley Swift, have provided a link with the white revolutionaries of the contemporary Fifth Era Klan, Aryan Nations, and Posse Comitatus. And Smith himself supported Christian Identity, the religious sect that now provides a religious underpinning for numerous far-right groups.

Identity Conflicts

Gerald L.K. Smith began life as a fundamentalist minister. By the Second World War, he had come to embrace an odd offshoot of Christian theology called Christian Identity, espoused by his friend and advance man, Wesley Swift.

Also known as British Israelism, Israel Identity, and Kingdom Message, the Christian Identity movement originated in Great Britain during the mid-nineteenth century. It is comprised of a loose collection of congregations that share the belief that white Christians are the true "Israelites" of the Old Testament, and are therefore God's chosen people — contrary to traditional Christian teaching, which assigns this role to the Jews.

According to Christian Identity, the ten lost tribes of Israel were the actual predecessors of Nordic, British, and American whites; modern-day Jews are descendants of a historically separate Kingdom of Judah. Great Britain became the modern-day Israel after the lost tribes travelled there via two great migration routes. One path led through Spain, into Scotland and Ireland, and from there to the current British ruling family — who are, of course, Lost Israelites.

Other tribes populated the rest of the white world, including America, which was settled by the Manasseh. The Manasseh was the thirteenth

tribe, and thirteen is a recurrent number in American custom: There were thirteen original colonies, thirteen stars and stripes on the first flag. On the official seal, there are thirteen stars in the glory cloud, thirteen bars in the escutcheon borne on the breast of the eagle and thirteen arrows clutched in its talon, thirteen letters in the motto *E pluribus unum*. Many Identity followers even came to regard American Indians as the true Aryan people. This fascination with Native Americans is also a long-standing Klan preoccupation: many Klansmen try to trace their heritage back through the blue eyes and finely chiselled features of certain American

Indian tribes, to the Celts, and, finally, to the lost tribes of Israel.

Odd as they might seem, the teachings of Christian Identity came to provide a fertile religious context for a revivified far right. The *New York Times* quoted Kurt Saxon, a survivalist and former American Nazi, on the significance of the Identity church: "It is like one great big club, and if you are on the run, a believer will shelter you regardless if he wears overt labels or not."

Rendered into modern political terms, Identity theory teaches that the U.S. is God's promised land and modern Israel a hoax. British followers of Identity are starkly anti-Semitic, but it was the American Identity theologians who added the ingeniously gnostic racist twist known as the "two seed" theory. They hold that the nonwhite races are "pre-Adamic" — that is, part of the creation finished *before* God created Adam and Eve. In his wisdom, they say, God fashioned the subhuman nonwhites and sent them to live outside the Garden of Eden before the Fall. When Eve broke God's original commandment, she was implanted with two seeds. From Adam's seed sprang Abel and the white race. From the serpent Satan's seed came the lazy, wicked Cain. Angered, God cast Adam, Eve, and the serpent out of the Garden of Eden and decreed eternal racial conflict. Cain killed Abel, then ran off into the jungle to join the pre-Adamic nonwhites. It's almost too neatly done: Identity theology provides both a religious base for racism and anti-Semitism, and an ideological rationale for violence against minorities and their white allies.

Identity followers have little use for fundamentalist Christians on the New Right (who, in turn, view Identity theory as heresy). The fundamentalist belief in "rapture" — the instant during the last days of the world when God will suddenly appear to protect his true believers and call them bodily into his presence — seems absurd to Identity worshippers. An Identity Christian isn't about to wait for God to save him; he puts more faith in a little direct political action. Flabby fundamentalism is regularly lampooned in pamphlets with titles like, "My minister, is he wrong AGAIN?" and "America's Jew-ridden New Right." For Christian Identity followers, the fundamentalists' support for Israel was the last nail on the coffin, making Jerry Falwell and Billy Graham into auxiliaries of the Jews.

Resurgence

CHAPTER 2

Resurgence

"King, look into your heart. You know you are a complete fraud and . . . like all frauds your end is approaching," the anonymous threat read. "You, even at an early age, have turned out to be not a leader but a dissolute, abnormal imbecile. . . . You are done. Your 'honorary' degrees, your Nobel Prize (what a grim farce) and other awards will not save you. King, I repeat you are done."

This letter, addressed to Dr. Martin Luther King, Jr., might have come from any one of his enemies on the far right. Instead, it was written at the highest levels of the Federal Bureau of Investigation and sent with the blessing of its director, J. Edgar Hoover, who viewed King as "one of the lowest characters in the country."

During the 1960s, the Klans not only enjoyed a resurgence, but also found new resonance in groups that sprang up to take advantage of an emotional new politics. Initially, this new trend was set off in reaction to the civil rights movement, but it came to include other strains from the American past: a quest for Puritan rectitude, suspicion of foreigners, and hatred of radicals. This revived nativism found a voice within the government itself in the form of the FBI's crusade against Martin Luther King, Jr.

Two Revolutions at Once

"In the most critical periods of our nation's history, there have always been those on the fringes of our society who have sought to escape their own responsibility by finding a simple solution, an appealing slogan or a convenient scapegoat," President John F. Kennedy said in his famous 1961 address on far-right conspiricists.

Financial crises could be explained by the presence of too many immigrants or too few greenbacks.

War could be attributed to munitions makers or international bankers. Peace conferences failed because we were duped by the British or tricked by the French or deceived by the Russians. . . .

Under the strains and frustrations imposed by constant tension and harassment, the discordant voices of extremism are heard once again in the land. Men who are unwilling to face up to the danger from without are convinced that the real danger comes from within.

They look suspiciously at their neighbors and their leaders. They call for 'a man on horseback' because they do not trust the people. They find treason in our finest churches, in our highest court and even in the treatment of our water. They equate the Democratic Party with the welfare state, the welfare state with socialism and socialism with communism. They object quite rightly to politics intruding on the military — but they are anxious for the military to engage in politics.

Kennedy was talking about the John Birch Society and the Minutemen, two groups on the far right that seemingly appeared out of nowhere in the 1960s as part of a political reaction to the civil rights revolution. Dismissed as kooks by most in society, they gave the raw energy and political context to a movement that would reshape the political arena. They made their mark on two presidential campaigns — Goldwater's and Wallace's — before eventually finding a mainstream political home in the presidency of Ronald Reagan. And they would eventually overshadow the Klan and change the face of nativist politics.

Founded in 1958, the John Birch Society was a secret group organized by Robert Welch, a Belmont, Massachusetts candy manufacturer, to save "our inheritance" from an "international communist plot." According to one brochure, "The long range objective of the Society has been summarized as less government, more responsibility, and a better world."

The organization imitated the Communist Party system: It was set up in cells called "chapters," and operated through myriad front groups, which aimed to penetrate organized political parties. They established propaganda centers in book stores, ran a lecture bureau, and published their own books and pamphlets.

Welch had little use for democratic institutions. In the *Blue Book*, the document in which he set forth the principles of the Society, Welch said democracy was "merely a deceptive phrase, a weapon of demagoguery, and a perennial fraud . . . the worst of all forms of government."

"This is a Republic, not a democracy," Welch said. "Let's keep it that way." And just to make the point clear, he wrote in the *Blue Book*: "The John Birch Society is to be a monolithic body. . . . The John Birch Society will operate under completely authoritative control at all levels. . . . It is imperative that all the strength we can muster be subject to smoothly functioning direction from the top. . . ."

A list of the governmental organizations the Birch Society opposed was all-encompassing: U.S. membership in the United Nations, the International Labor Organization, the International Trade Organization, the World Health Organization, UNICEF, the General Agreement on Tariffs and Trade, and NATO. It opposed "so-called defense spending," all foreign aid, and diplomatic relations with the Soviet Union and other communist nations. It was against the National Labor Relations Act, social security, the graduated income tax, the Reconstruction Finance Corporation, the Tennessee Valley Authority, government wage and price controls, "forced integration," U.S. government bonds, the Federal Reserve System, urban renewal, water fluoridation, the corporate dividend tax, the "mental health" racket, federal aid to housing, and all programs "regimenting farmers." Welch invented the term "Comsymp." ("You don't have to tell how much they are Communists and how much sympathizers.")

By 1966, membership in the John Birch Society had grown to 80,000 individuals in 5,000 different chapters across the country — making it about equal to membership in the American Communist Party in the early 1940s. An all-out attack on the civil rights movement became the major focus of the Birch Society. Welch wrote a document entitled *Two Revolutions at Once* and had 500,000 copies sent out to Birchers around the country. "Our task," the pamphlet said, "must be simply to make clear that the movement known as 'civil rights' is Communist-plotted, Communist-controlled, and in fact . . . serves only Communist purposes. So let's keep our activities and efforts concentrated on this central undertaking."

The Birch Society set up front groups called TACT — Truth About Civil Turmoil — committees, which posed as black support groups. Among the members were right-wing blacks, including a former communist informant for the FBI. In 1965, the Birch Society journal *American Opinion* described what happened at the civil rights march in Selma, "when a horde of termites from all over the country, led by half-crazed ministers and professors, swarmed over the small town of Selma, Ala., in a typical demonstration of Communist activism." After the Watts riots of 1967, Birch chapters across the country were mobilized to launch intensive anti–civil rights drives, playing to white fear.

Welch liked to look back to the Jim Crow days of his childhood on a North Carolina farm, when there was, he said, "a huge reservoir of good will between the races," and "a very, very tiny amount of injustice." In their analysis of the race question, Birch publications relied on the writings of the segregationist White Citizens' Councils.

The Birch Society claimed Kluxers were not welcome in the organization. But as the Anti-Defamation League pointed out, Birchers and Kluxers frequently intermingled. On September 13, 1965, at the Henry Grady Hotel in Atlanta, retired Major General Edwin A. Walker, long a proud member of the Birch Society, said to resounding cheers, "There will be a KKK in the USA longer than there will be an LBJ." And it was Walker, in an earlier speech in Long Beach, California, who put his finger on the heart of the sentiment that linked anti-communism with a racist imperative. The communist conspiracy, he warned, was aimed at "you, the white race," poised for action "just ninety miles from Florida."

As for anti-Semitism, Welch insisted over and over again he was not anti-Semitic. Instead he related the subject to the overall communist plot in a novel way, declaring:

> Anti-Semitism has been the most powerful weapon the Communists have had at different times. In my opinion — I think you could prove it — anti-Semitism was created by the Communists for them to be able to use both sides. There was some hatred or dislike for Jews still left in Europe in the latter part of the 19th century but not much. In America, practically none . . .
>
> I have not the slightest doubt that 'The Protocols of the Elders of Zion,' which has been

used so extensively and disastrously to create trouble, was written either by Lenin or for Lenin deliberately to serve their purposes in many ways.

There is no doubt, in my opinion, that it was a Communist who twisted Henry Ford, Sr., into making such a dope of himself in his book and so forth, and creating situations that would make him so angry and cause him to do these things. And the Communists used that. . . .

While Welch warned against anti-Semitism, he nonetheless thought Jews had their own hand in the communist plot. "There came a period of some forty years when an abnormal percentage of the visible leadership of the Communist conspiracy was of Jewish ancestry," he wrote in the November 1965 Birch Society bulletin. "And these traitors to their race — as well as to all mankind — worked and schemed and plotted to have themselves hated, not as Communists, but as Jews."

As for Welch himself, Frank P. Mintz, in his book *The Liberty Lobby and the American Right*, suggests that Welch was less spooked by the Jews than he was by a group he called the "Insiders," who, he believed, constituted a modern version of the old Illuminati. In a 1964 speech, Welch discussed history as a contest between good and evil, and cited the Illuminati as a force for evil. The Insiders, in Welch's world view, had apparently absorbed the communists. They used the communists, along with anarchists, socialists, opportunistic politicians, idealists, and others, to get ahead. To advance their scheme, they backed the advance of government at the expense of individual rights, through such initiatives as the Federal Reserve System, the income tax, and the direct election of congressmen. The Insiders had also financed Lenin and Trotsky to gain a footing in Russia.

Such an all-encompassing conspiracy theory raised eyebrows on the right. The *National Review* had once welcomed the John Birch Society on the scene, but grew to distance itself from the Birchers. What hurt Welch on the right more than anything was his characterization of President Eisenhower as a communist. In his book *The Politician*, he had written scathingly of the president's brother Milton, calling him "an outright Communist" and adding that in "my firm belief . . . Dwight Eisenhower is a dedicated conscious agent of the Communist conspiracy."

Unlike the far-right groups of the 1980s, Mintz notes, the John Birch Society was not actively revolutionary. Welch never advocated not paying taxes and never argued for overthrow of the government. But there is little doubt that the group sheltered others of a far more activist mien. One of them was Robert DePugh, founder of the Minutemen.

On Target

The son of a sheriff in a Kansas City suburb, DePugh was a stateside radar man in the Second World War. He studied chemistry and genetics in college, but never graduated. He thought the radar scientists he came in contact with in the army were disloyal, and couldn't figure out why everyone was picking on Senator Joseph McCarthy. DePugh found out just how far down the drain into "communism" America had gone when his veterinary chemical company went bankrupt and he had to deal with the government's nightmare of red tape.

"The Minutemen are a national organization of patriotic Americans who are preparing themselves as a last line of defense against communism," reads a booklet explaining the purpose of the group. It continues:

Minutemen founder Robert DePugh (left), with his first lieutenant, Walter Peyson, after appearing in Federal District Court in Spokane, Washington in 1969. They had attended a hearing on charges they conspired to rob four banks to raise money for their private right-wing army.

Our diplomatic war against communism has already been lost by bunglers or traitors within our own government. . . . A pro-American government can no longer be established by normal political means. There has not been one presidential election since World War II where the American public has had an opportunity to vote for a real American. There have been times when the candidates were built up by big public relations campaigns that sold them to the American people but when they were once in office they failed to act in their nation's best interest. Even the defeated candidates for president have shown by subsequent events to be little or not better than those elected.

The Minutemen dedicated themselves to underground guerrilla tactics, forming secret squads and supposedly becoming technical masterminds in electronics, secret inks, demolition, and chemical and biological warfare. As DePugh told William Turner, who interviewed him for a 1966 article in *Ramparts*, "We have the most sophisticated and best equipped underground army movement this world has ever seen." He told another interviewer that the super secret membership lists of the organization were bottled in a nitroglycerin mixture that would explode on opening.

Whether or not DePugh's men indeed ever mastered any of the advanced technical aspects of warfare which have eluded most of the other guerrilla armies in the world, they did hit on one surefire means of building an army: the National Rifle Association, through which they became eligible for free ammunition and at-cost surplus weapons from the government's Office of Civilian Marksmanship. The FBI dismissed the Minutemen's claim to a membership of 80,000, and J. Edgar Hoover labeled the group a "paper organization." Yet the extraordinary arsenals built up by Minutemen in different states during the 1960s became a serious problem for state and local law enforcement officials for years to come. In Illinois in 1964, to cite but one example, undercover investigators found one Minuteman offering for sale $17,000-worth of sophisticated weapons, including a 75-millimeter recoilless rifle, .50 caliber machine guns, submachine guns, mortars, and other assorted arms.

To identify the enemy for the guerrilla army, Minutemen were told to find the communist enemy within and harass them — to which end DePugh built a file on 65,000 individuals at his Norborne, Missouri headquarters, and named 1,500 members of the "communist hidden government" who would be targeted for assassination in the event of a coup.

"Generally the hardest working members of the John Birch Society are members of the Minutemen," DePugh once said, explaining how Minutemen were urged to join other right-wing organizations to ensure that the group's values and tactics were extended throughout the movement. DePugh himself, however, was run out of the John Birch Society when he started the Minutemen.

The Minutemen embraced various offshoots from the radical right. "Twenty American Nazis were absorbed en masse, although DePugh insists it was with the stipulation that they conform to Minutemen standards," Turner wrote in *Ramparts*. "The Ku Klux Klanners abound, and there is a clutch of National States Rights Party adherents. The Minutemen coordinator for Pennsylvania, Roy Frankhauser, Jr., and his New Jersey counterpart, Frank Rotella, are better known for their roles of state Grand Dragons of the Klan."

For a time in the late 1960s, DePugh sheltered most of the nation's paramilitary groups under the Minutemen umbrella — including the Sons of Liberty in New Jersey, the Christian Soldiers in St. Louis, and the Paul Revere Associated Yeomen in New Orleans. The largest Minutemen group, Turner speculated, was the Soldiers of the Cross, an Englewood, Colorado outfit whose leader, Rev. Kenneth Goff, sat on the Minutemen national council. Goff, a former communist, had hooked up with far-right figure Gerald L.K. Smith, and his group advanced the theory that the Soviets were secretly buying up horses along the West Coast in order to mount a Cossack-style attack on California and beyond. Another group affiliated with the Minutemen was Dr. Wesley Swift's Church of Jesus Christ Christian, which evolved into the Aryan Nations.

Swift, in turn, was allied with the late Colonel William Gale, who had been an aide to General MacArthur in the Pacific during the Second World War. In the 1960s Gale was a leader of the paramilitary California Rangers and later became a Christian Identity preacher. Gale was a dedicated anti-Semite, saying, "You got your nigger Jews, you got your Asiatic Jews and you got your white Jews. They're all Jews, and they're all the offspring of the devil." Another of Swift's ministers was Connie Lynch, a wild-eyed Klansman and Christian Identity preacher.

President Kennedy incensed the Minutemen, who attacked him in their publication *On Target*. The newsletter also ran an item addressed to twenty "Judas" members of Congress who voted to abolish the House Un-American Activities Committee: "See the old man at the corner where you buy your papers: He may have a silencer-equipped pistol under his coat. That extra fountain pen in the pocket of the insurance salesman that calls on you might be a cyanide gas gun. . . . These [Minutemen] patriots are not going to let you take their freedom. They have learned the silent knife, the strangler's cord, the target rifle that hits sparrows at 200 yards. Only their leaders restrain them. Traitors beware! Even now the cross-hairs are on the back of your necks."

The Minutemen attempted to assassinate Arkansas Senator William Fulbright, a ranking member of the Democratic Party who was chairman of the Senate Foreign Relations Committee. Other Minutemen embarked on a failed plan to attack the United Nations by poisoning its ventilation system with cyanide. And the Kennedy assassination never fazed the Minutemen; their publication announced, "We will not soon forget that he ignored the best interest of his country from the day he took office to the day he died. . . ."

Carto's Imperative

Among Welch's early supporters was Willis Carto, one of the most enduring, if mysterious, figures in post-war far-right history. From the 1960s on, he sought to stitch together a racialist — and what he insisted on calling "populist" — political coalition within the conservative movement. He was active on the fringes of both the Goldwater and the Wallace campaigns. During the 1980s he organized a third party, the Populist Party, in an effort to attract the far-right fringe of the Reagan revolution.

Carto is an elusive figure, writing under different pseudonyms, seldom photographed, and rarely granting interviews. Born in Fort Wayne, Indiana in 1926, he entered the military after graduating from high school, and returned to the U.S. after World War II to take a job as a bill collector for Household Finance in San Francisco. In his early days Carto appeared to be a conservative of the libertarian school. He became active in right-wing circles on the West Coast, creating his own small group, Liberty and Property, and its monthly bulletin, *Right*.

From the beginning, *Right* described and attacked an establishment of bankers, big businessmen, foundations, Zionists, and Jewish organizations such as the Anti-Defamation League. The November 1956 *Right* described the interests supporting the Eisenhower administration as "internationalist millionaires," many of whom were "closely associated with the big international banks which have brought so much grief to the world by their financing of the Russian Bolshevik revolution and their successful agitation for wars which have all but destroyed Western civilization."

Right was openly anti-Semitic and anti-Zionist. It supported the defendants in the 1942 pro-Axis sedition trials, and in the late 1950s backed the new racist, paramilitary National States Rights Party, led by Edward Fields. In one *Right* article, American Nazi leader George Lincoln Rockwell declared, "And dangerous we ARE. To Jew traitors we are deadly and we openly inform them

we will stuff them into gas chambers in 1972 when we are elected to power."

Later in the 1950s, Carto joined the John Birch Society, but departed after less than a year, after getting into a spat with founder Robert Welch. Then in August 1957, *Right* announced the formation of the Liberty Lobby, which, it said, would serve as a bridge between "patriots" and Congress, providing research and gathering news for "patriots and conservative groups."

From the start the Liberty Lobby had a strongly xenophobic and racialist bent. It also attacked the moderate, internationalist wing of the Republican Party — which even then was on the defensive — and advocated a free enterprise "populist" economy. As Mintz explains, while it engaged in endless squabbles with different groups on the right, the Liberty Lobby joined in the general drive to keep the Republican Party under the Goldwater wing. And indeed, its fortunes rose with those of Goldwater. One measure of the Liberty Lobby's growth was the popularity of its newsletter, the *Liberty Letter*, whose purported circulation rose from 16,000 in 1963 to 200,000 by 1967.

Throughout the 1960s, the Liberty Lobby published a stream of books, pamphlets, and newsletters, and provided testimony to Congress on topics of the day. A Liberty Lobby representative testified at a 1967 hearing on the omnibus civil rights bill, arguing the line of "Negro immaturity" — claiming that blacks were a "younger" race than whites with lighter brains and less developed frontal lobes. Overall, the Liberty Lobby urged conservatives to identify with the segregationist South, and harped on the alliance between international bankers and world communism.

As the civil rights campaign marched toward its popular victory, and the conservative movement emerged from Goldwater's nomination in San Francisco's Cow Palace in 1964, the Liberty Lobby argued that the Republicans could offset Democratic gains among blacks with a new approach. *Looking Forward*, a Liberty Lobby position paper subtitled "Study of the New Trend within the Conservative Movement," was published in March 1965. It provided a sober assessment of the 1964 presidential election, and sketched the future terrain:

A factor pushing the Republican Party into being the natural vehicle for the expression of 'White

Rights' is the inevitable movement of the Democratic party in the South toward becoming an all-Black party.

One of the tragedies of Conservatism is that there is so little realistic political thinking within its ranks. For example, Conservatives have allowed the Left to manufacture an obscene and repulsive. hobgoblin out of the constructive and pathetic appeal of Negroes for racial self-expression, dignity and independence. We speak, of course, not of the fraudulent assimilation movement, which is rapidly creating a state of total chaos and anarchy in many areas of America, but of the contrasting movement of responsible Negro nationalism represented in the public mind now, unfortunately, by an assortment of wild-eyed crackpots and Communists. Even while this misrepresentation continues, however, the way is being prepared for a genuine fulfillment of the fervent desires of Abraham Lincoln, Thomas Jefferson, James Madison and true Negro leaders like Marcus Garvey, all of whom envisioned an end to centuries of racial strife through mutual recognition of the need for racial separation. Exploitation of this basically commendable and honorable movement has, as we know, been made by Communists which exhibits an uncanny ability to seek out and exploit the most basic urges of all people. We would ask if this is primarily because Conservatives have failed to evaluate properly this movement (ever since the assassination of Abraham Lincoln) and failed to take advantage.

The authors of *Looking Forward* were encouraged by George Wallace's campaign, but discarded the idea of organizing a third party around the Alabama governor in favor of what it called "The party-within-a-party concept." Rather than make an end run on the two-party system, conservatives would actively organize to elect conservatives in every congressional district.

Carto never got along with the other sectors of the evolving right that were beginning to coalesce in Republican politics. William Buckley's

National Review attacked Carto as a racist whacko. And while Robert Welch of the John Birch Society shared Carto's and the Liberty Lobby's conspiracist theories of history, the two men differed fundamentally on the source of the conspiracy. Welch had no sympathy for anti-Semitism, and dismissed the idea that Jewish bankers were behind the purported communist grab for power. Instead, he believed that the communists were backed by the fiendish and extraordinarily long-lived Illuminati.

In 1968 the Liberty Lobby leaped into organized politics, taking control of the Youth for Wallace organization. In its new guise, Youth for Wallace became the National Youth Alliance.

But the National Youth Alliance soon split up. One of its splinters, the National Alliance, followed William Pierce, the Oregon physics professor who had previously been employed taping hate messages for American Nazi leader George Lincoln Rockwell. Pierce would go on to write the manifesto of the white underground, a novel called *Turner Diaries*, which later inspired Robert Mathews and the Order in their effort to build a white bastion in the American Northwest. The National Alliance spawned a full litter of racist revolutionaries in the early 1980s.

The Liberty Lobby also prospered, and in the 1970s began running a network of radio stations. In August 1975, the *Liberty Letter* was replaced by the *Spotlight*, a weekly tabloid that sought to appeal to many factions on the right. In October 1975, *Spotlight* wrote enthusiastically of new directions in the Ku Klux Klan, heralded by the emergence of David Duke, who was young, university-educated, and "smart as a tack." By 1981, the *Spotlight* boasted a circulation of 250,000.

The emergence of Ronald Reagan both elevated nativism to new heights and cut off political organizing outside the mainstream of the Republi-

can Party, which by the 1980s was firmly in the hands of a New Right coalition. The new president was comfortable with much of the conspiracist thinking that had marked the fulminations of the Liberty Lobby and the John Birch Society.

Hitler's Lenin

Although Nazism never seriously took root in the U.S., any account of the far right needs a mention of George Lincoln Rockwell.

In the 1920s, the Ku Klux Klan had set up a klavern — a membership group with regular meetings — in Germany. Hitler himself claimed to have been inspired by Henry Ford; and William Dudley Pelley and Gerald B. Winrod at one time or another embraced Hitler. Any number of isolationist politicians had urged the U.S. to stay out of the Second World War, and for a brief period the American Nazi Party and the Klan had struck a merger. But after the war Nazism was an alien element on the far right. George Lincoln Rockwell reversed all that, establishing by himself a small Nazi movement that became enmeshed in the politics of far-right groups of the 1950s and 1960s. Today he is, curiously, looked back on as a seminal figure in the Aryan movement.

Rockwell was the son of a vaudeville comedian, and was schooled in New England, attending Hebron Academy and Brown University before launching into a promising career as an advertising illustrator. He was a Navy pilot in World War II, then was recalled to duty in Korea, which helped to enrich his anti-communist sentiments. Like many of the other post-war rightist figures, Rockwell somewhere along the way heard a rousing speech by Gerald L.K. Smith, which sent him racing out to buy a copy of *Mein Kampf*.

During the 1950s, Rockwell whipped up anti-communism through an organization called the Die Hards, then through another group called the American Federation of Conservative Organizations (AFCO). He wrote for the rightist *American Mercury*, and supported Joe McCarthy. He worked for the United White Party and then joined the National Committee to Free America from Jewish Domination. Eventually, Rockwell turned his Arlington, Virginia house into the headquarters of the American Nazi Party.

Rockwell's gift was a flamboyance that brought the Nazi Party — which probably never had more than a few thousand members — a measure of public attention far beyond any measure of its power. Americans watched while he announced

American Nazi Party leader George Lincoln Rockwell, as he addresses a 1966 rally of 1,500 white people in Chicago.

his determination to exterminate Jewish traitors — which he estimated to number 80 percent of all Jews — and to send all blacks back to Africa. Wherever he went — whether it was to New York, where Mayor Robert Wagner argued that he shouldn't be permitted to speak, or to Boston, where he picketed the film *Exodus* and theatergoers pelted him with stones and eggs — he stirred up controversy. He was denied entrance into Australia. Skirting a ban on his visit by the British government by slipping into the country from Ireland, Rockwell was immediately deported.

Rockwell toured the South in a bus which carried a big sign saying, "We hate Jew Communism," and picketed the *Exodus* screenings with a placard that read, "America for Whites and Gas Chamber for Traitors." He picketed both black activists and white conservatives, and mocked Jews whenever he got a chance. Eventually he was arrested and charged with disorderly conduct. Defended by a Jewish lawyer and appearing before a black judge, Rockwell was released on $100 bail, and eventually acquitted in a trial where attorneys argued over his right to free speech. On August 25, 1967, Rockwell was shot and killed by his lieutenant, John Patler, in the parking lot of an Arlington laundromat. After a series of stormy confrontations, he was buried with military honors.

The American Nazi movement had never been especially large — at its height, it had no more than 2,000 members — and following Rockwell, it broke into various factions. But with the passage of time and the emergence of an internationally minded rightist movement, the Nazis and Rockwell have gained in stature in the annals of the American right.

Rising Again

During the early 1960s, the old-style Ku Klux Klan was overshadowed by the Birchers and the Minutemen, the new players on the American far right who caught the attention of the media. But the Klan saw itself unfairly bearing the frontline struggle in a new era of radical reconstruction in the South. Kennedy's election revived the Klan's old papist hatred, but that soon gave way to a new sense of desperation and dread as Greyhound buses filled with white and black kamikaze college students calling themselves Freedom Riders descended upon the South. After 1960 Klan membership doubled to 20,000 (still paltry by 1920s standards). But the numbers scarcely tell the story.

As the civil rights movement went forward, it was faced with the greatest surge of violent backlash since the Klan's formation after the Civil War. In Birmingham, Alabama, two dozen Klansmen beat Freedom Riders with pipes as they arrived to challenge the segregation of bus stations and restaurants. In Montgomery, another Klan-led mob met them with clubs and pipes. Attorney General Robert Kennedy dispatched 500 marshals to Montgomery and sought an injunction against the Klan.

Confronted with this invasion by marshals and civil rights workers, the various Klans held a meeting in Georgia. Their goal was to overcome their differences and they merged into a new organization, the United Klans of America, headed by a young newcomer, thirty-two-year-old Bobby Shelton. Shelton quickly became the most visible leader of the largest Klan conglomeration in the nation. He disliked communism and foreign-made goods, and was a stout Methodist. "I don't hate niggers," he is quoted by Wyn Craig Wade in *The Fiery Cross*. "But I hate the Jews. The nigger's a child, but the Jews are dangerous people. . . . All

Imperial Wizard Robert Shelton addresses a United Klans rally in Tuscaloosa, Alabama on April 4, 1965.

Klanspeak

Empire. *The national Ku Klux Klan organization.*
Realm. *The Klan in a particular state.*
Dominion. *Five or more counties of a Realm.*
Province. *One to three counties in a Dominion.*
Klanton or Den. *Local chapter.*
Klavern. *Local meeting place.*
Imperial Wizard. *Head of national Ku Klux Klan.*
Grand Dragon. *Head of a Realm.*
Great Titan. *Head of a Dominion.*
Giant. *Head of a Province.*
Exalted Cyclops. *Head of a Klanton.*
Klaliff. *Vice president to Exalted Cyclops.*
Kladd. *Assistant Exalted Cyclops.*
Kleagle. *An organizer.*
Kludd. *Chaplain.*
Klokard. *National lecturer.*

they want is control and domination of the Gentiles through a conspiracy with the niggers." Shelton thought all Jews were communists. To gain wider popular support, he downplayed anti-black and anti-Jewish sentiment, stressing instead the communist influence in the civil rights movement.

In retrospect it now seems to have been a losing battle, but the Klan fought every inch of the way. Klansmen were among the rioters who opposed black student James Meredith's enrollment at the University of Mississippi — achieved only after the arrival of National Guard and federal troops. When Dr. Martin Luther King, Jr. began demonstrations in Birmingham, police chief Bull Conner, in sympathy with the Klan, attacked the crowds. Klansmen were thought to be responsible for bombs that blew up a hotel that King had just left, as well as the home of King's brother. George Wallace, who promised to stand fast for segregation, was a Klan hero, and employed a former top Klansman as his personal adviser. Klansmen were also implicated in the bombing of the Sixteenth Street Baptist Church in Birmingham, where four young black girls were killed (though it was not until 1977 that a Klansman was tried and convicted on charges of first-degree murder for the bombing).

Christian Identity minister Charles Conley (Connie) Lynch, the self-styled "Jap killer," led a particularly vicious Klan in St. Augustine, Florida. As Wade notes, Lynch was an early exponent of Christian Identity. He also belonged to DePugh's Minutemen, along with such other ministers as Wesley Swift and Bill Gale. At one rally Lynch whipped up the crowd with his own style of Christian Identity invective. He demanded to know why people should feel sorry for the black girls killed in the Birmingham church. "They weren't children," he said. "Children are little people, little human beings, and that means white people. . . . There's little dogs and cats and apes and baboons and skunks and there's also little niggers. But they ain't children. They're just little niggers." When the Kluxers spied four black men watching the rally, Lynch pulled a pistol, and the crowd descended on the blacks, beating them with fists and gun butts. By the time the police arrived the mob was getting ready to burn the black men alive.

Lynch and the other perpetrators of this near-lynching got off. It was the murders of Michael Schwerner, Andrew Goodman, and James Chaney by the Klan in Philadelphia, Mississippi that marked a change in the way the nation viewed the Klan — in part because, for the first time, J. Edgar Hoover took it seriously. When the three civil

rights workers — two white and one black — disappeared, Hoover sent in 153 agents, with 400 Naval troops to assist them. The diligence of the FBI, the blanketing of Neshoba County by the press, and the evidence of collusion by the local police in the murders dramatically changed people's attitudes. The revelations aroused students on northern college campuses and ignited black rage in Harlem and in other cities across the North. In July 1964, Congress passed and President Johnson signed into law the Civil Rights Act.

But the perpetrators of the Schwerner, Chaney, and Goodman murders initially escaped punishment, as did other accused Klansmen, and Klan violence continued: Klansmen shot to death Lemuel A. Penna, a black Army reservist, as he drove back to his home in Washington, D.C. from a two-week tour of duty at Fort Benning. The Klan burned churches across Louisiana, a funeral home in North Carolina, a Freedom School in Mississippi. Two black youths were injured by shotguns fired from passing cars. Then, on March 25, 1965, a Klan hit team ran across Viola Liuzzo, a white woman from Detroit who was in Selma for the civil rights march, as she drove a black teenaged boy in her car. They chased her at high speed and, drawing even, opened fire, killing her instantly.

While nationwide there was a general dislike for the idea of northern "carpetbaggers" going into the South, the Klan's violence and seeming invulnerability to prosecution eventually helped the civil rights movement. Just as Congress had passed the Civil Rights Act shortly after the killings of Schwerner, Chaney, and Goodman, the Voting Rights Act was enacted into law in the aftermath of the Liuzzo murder.

J. Edgar Hoover and Martin Luther King, Jr.

It was easy enough to dismiss George Lincoln Rockwell as a huckster or Robert DePugh as a fringe conspiracist. And the Klan's rigid, stifling ideology could not support anything but a narrow and defensive, if violent, rear guard. But many people, in the North as well as in the South, thought the Freedom Riders were asking for it, pushing the South too far too fast, and while they would never buy the trappings of the Birch Society and the whacko theories of Welch, many in the early 1960s agreed that the black civil rights movement might well be an instrument of subversive international communism.

The leaders of the country were heedful of such sentiments. John and Robert Kennedy believed in the Cold War, and both were highly alert to the possibilities of communist meddling in domestic affairs. They were especially concerned when the FBI brought them evidence that a close confidant of Martin Luther King, Jr. had been a high figure in the U.S. Communist Party.

The FBI's investigation of King and other civil rights leaders fit into a historic agenda. Beginning with the Palmer Raids of 1919, what was then called the Bureau of Investigation, through its General Intelligence Division, had kept an eye out for agitation among the Negro population. Among the Bureau's earliest concerns was protection of the American public from radical groups which "bored from within." In 1919 and again in 1920 a young J. Edgar Hoover sent special reports on "agitation" within the Negro community to the attorney general and the Senate, and his agents reported that radicals were working "industriously to disaffect the Negroes of the United States." At first, blame was placed on the Industrial Workers of the World. When the American Communist Party was formed, it quickly became the culprit. The Bureau told Congress that blacks were "appealed to directly by propagandists of the Communist parties for support in the movement to overthrow the government of the United States." And it reported that "The reds have done a vast amount of evil damage by carrying doctrines of race revolt and the poison of Bolshevism to the Negroes," and that "this business has been perhaps the most contemptible and wicked performance of our American revolutionary fanatics."

The FBI detectives read articles in the black press that supported civil rights and opposed lynchings; they found the articles impertinent, and as a result the Bureau placed undercover agents in meetings of black organizations. Worried by the call for blacks to organize, Hoover believed he saw the hand of the communists at work. After the race riots of 1919 he reported to Congress, "Thus we see the cause of much of the racial trouble in the United States at the present time. . . . The Communist party of America . . . is . . . pledged . . . to stir up and agitate racial prejudices throughout the entire country."

Over forty years later, an FBI informant was among the Klansmen who organized the 1961 attack on the Freedom Riders. He reported both the plan for the attack and the police's role in it to his FBI contact. The FBI did nothing to stop the attack, and its silent complicity was not revealed until fourteen years later.

FBI agents also had eyewitnesses who had seen two members of the Klan at Birmingham's Sixteenth Street Baptist Church eight hours before the bombings there. But when the agents notified Washington, Hoover dissuaded them from taking action, noting that the chances for any successful prosecution were remote. Five months later, the Birmingham agents thought they had enough evidence to convict one of the Klansmen. Again Hoover refused, warning the agents to keep quiet lest the matter get into the press — thereby, of course, fueling the civil rights movement.

When President Lyndon B. Johnson was informed of the Liuzzo murder, he decided to launch a full investigation of the Klan, and to push for new legislation against it. But Hoover insisted that the Bureau was doing everything it could on the Klan front, and urged him not to make too much of the Liuzzo affair. In an FBI memo that lay hidden for twenty years, Hoover recounted a conversation with LBJ: "I stated Jim [Liuzzo] doesn't have too good a background and the woman [Viola] had indications of needle marks in her arms where she had been taking dope; that she was sitting very, very close to the Negro in the car; that it had the appearance of a necking party."

Necking during a hundred-mile-an-hour car chase is hard to imagine. And the coroner's report contradicted Hoover's claim.

But as it turned out, these were signs of larger and more ominous events, which in recent years have been exhaustively explored by David J. Garrow in his book *The FBI and Martin Luther King, Jr.* Garrow's findings show that from the late 1950s onward, the FBI had spied on Stanley Levison, a former member of the Communist Party. When the Bureau discovered that Levison was also a friend and close adviser to Martin Luther King, Jr. and the Southern Christian Leadership Conference, J. Edgar Hoover notified President Kennedy and Attorney General Robert Kennedy. Both approved Hoover's requests for wiretaps of Levison and King. Those wiretaps, and periodic surveillance of King, were maintained until 1965. Both

Greyhound bus, carrying an integrated group of Freedom Riders, bombed by a mob of white segregationists after being stopped in Anniston, Alabama in 1961.

Kennedys worried that King could come under the influence of foreign communism, and on various occasions the administration sought to alert King to a possible danger. The administration became more alarmed when it found that another close King adviser, Jack Odell, had once been affiliated with the Communist Party. To the FBI the smoke grew thicker when Levison quit his open association with King, but continued it through a third party. As for Odell, although he formally resigned his post at the SCLC, the FBI surveillance revealed that he continued to work for them.

After President Kennedy's assassination, the nature of the Bureau's surveillance changed, becoming less concerned with any possible connection to foreign communism than with King's political and personal objectives. As Garrow reveals, Hoover provided President Johnson with detailed reports from surveillance done during the civil rights movement's challenge to the Democratic Party at its 1964 Atlantic City convention. And his pursuit of King began to grow more and more obsessive.

The history of Hoover's conservative political views is well established, as are his undoubtedly racist sentiments. When it came to Martin Luther King, Jr., Hoover was also influenced by what his wiretaps and surveillance revealed about King's frisky personal life; it made him all the more determined to destroy King. Hoover's feelings were further inflamed by King's just accusations that the FBI had not hired any blacks to speak of, and that the southern agents had shown little enthusiasm for prosecuting Klansmen and other perpetrators of crimes against civil rights workers — especially in Albany, Georgia, where the lead agent was a well-known racist. To neutralize King, the Bureau sent repeated memoranda to top government officials from the president on down, always reasserting the supposed communist influences in the SCLC, but then providing intimate details of King's personal life. They offered pictures, transcripts of tapes, and other information to various newspaper reporters, and even attempted to influence the Swedish government when King was given the Nobel Peace Prize. At one point a top FBI official wrote an anonymous threatening letter to King, enclosing a copy of a surreptitious tape recording. It arrived at SCLC headquarters and fell into the hands of Mrs. King.

Garrow asserts that after King and various other civil rights leaders came out against the Vietnam War, LBJ became an ever-eager recipient of information about King. And at the time King was shot in Memphis in 1968, the FBI was at work trying to discredit his labor organizing, fearing what would result from the upcoming Poor People's March in Washington.

These actions by the FBI -– authorized, and in the case of Kennedy, actually initiated, by the president — reflect precisely the same xenophobic and nativist tendencies Kennedy himself had attacked in his famous speech about the John Birch Society and the Minutemen. In fact, the FBI never uncovered any evidence linking the communists to King or to the SCLC, yet the paranoid surveillance had continued for years. While Robert Welch's and Robert DePugh's fears of communist conspiracy were far more explicit and overwrought than those of the Kennedy brothers, they were all very much the product of Cold War thinking. And Hoover's obsession with King's personal life was just another manifestation of the puritan urge that had fueled the far right since the 1920s — since the days of the Klan's alliance with Protestant fundamentalism. Hoover's conservatism, his desire to turn the clock back to a more tranquil era, his well-known suspicion of foreign radicals — which had provided a motivation for the FBI since its formation after the Palmer Raids — all are reflections of American culture. There is nothing especially sinister about agents of the Federal Bureau of Investigation; they are products of the society that employs them. But the FBI, in turn, has helped to develop and propagate in the United States the conspiracist view of history, with far more success than Robert Welch or Robert DePugh ever dreamed of achieving.

Into the Political Arena

While politicians long eschewed any formal involvement with most of the so-called fringe groups on the far right, these groups nonetheless provided the energy — and in some instances the political expertise and manpower — for mainstream politics.

They were the roar behind Goldwater at the 1964 Republican convention in San Francisco, and Goldwater never turned his back on the Birchers, even after Welch's far-out remark about Ike. DePugh also promised to work for Goldwater, turning loose his purported army of 25,000 Minutemen to infiltrate and sabotage LBJ's campaign.

They turned out in unexpectedly large numbers to put George Wallace on the ballot in the northern industrial blue-collar states of Indiana and Wisconsin in 1964. In 1968 and 1972 Birchers, along with other conservatives, went for Wallace, and the Klan in certain states provided an infrastructure for the Alabama governor's campaign. When Robert Sherrill of the *Nation* magazine asked Wallace in 1968, "You'll get most of your support from the right wing, I suppose. Why don't you dissociate yourself from the kooks if you want to be taken seriously?" Wallace replied, "Well, Kennedy and Lyndon Johnson got support from the *Daily Worker*. Why didn't they disavow that? . . . I don't know who hammers up my posters. But I appreciate all the help I can get." He went on: "Some of the people out soliciting help for us aren't authorized to do it, but I'm not criticizing them. I will determine the issues and the platform and the way we run our campaign; they won't. We've got some of the finest folks in the country writing us letters, encouraging us, legislators in a great number of states, people in local Democrat and Republican committees telling us they will vote for us no matter what ticket we run on: bankers, businessmen, officials — not high up, you know, in local labor unions." Later Bill Jones, Wallace's campaign manager, told Sherrill, "We'd refuse Gus Hall's support in a minute, but it isn't that easy with [Klan leader Bobby] Shelton's support."

By 1976, the political energy on the right was a growing tidal wave. Wherever Ronald Reagan went during his primary contest with Gerald Ford, lines of voters would form at the town meetings staged by his campaign, and the questions would begin: What about the Trilateral Commission? What about a return to the gold standard? When will you take off the gloves with Castro? When will you get the government out of education, off the back of business, out of the United Nations, put a stop to busing? From the beginning, Reagan played to resurgent conservatism, to nationalism, and to fundamentalism — the emerging foundations of the New Right. But he also played to the fringes, taking the ground held first by Goldwater, then by Wallace.

The
Fifth
Era

CHAPTER 3

The Fifth Era

A s the long line of cars and trucks rolled through the Greensboro, North Carolina housing project in 1979, there were shouts of "Death to the Klan," and then, "Niggers, kikes . . ." A fight broke out; suddenly, there were shots, as Nazis and Klansmen opened fire on protesting members of the Communist Workers Party, killing five and wounding nine others.

Organized by a group of Ku Klux Klans, the Greensboro massacre became the best known in a series of escalating outbursts of racial violence by what was coming to be known as the "white resistance." This resistance movement was different from any that had come before, representing a coming together of previously independent, often quarrelsome groups on the far right. The Greensboro massacre was the work of the Klan, but members of the Klan cavalcade were also linked to neo-Nazis groups and to the Aryan Nations. All of these groups, and their leaders, would from then on be interconnected. For the first time, it was possible to see the outlines of a new phase in the far-right movement, which would come to be known as the Fifth Era.

Robert Miles in front of his Michigan farm.

The Old Man
of the Mountain

The earliest stirrings of this new movement were to be found in George Wallace's 1968 presidential campaign, and in the activities of one of his most ardent supporters, Robert Miles. A former Detroit insurance executive and member of the Michigan Republican Party, Robert Miles had quit the party after the Detroit race riots of 1967, gone in with George Wallace, and joined the Ku Klux Klan, eventually becoming grand dragon.

Miles was born in Bridgeport, Connecticut in 1925. The son of an auto worker — Miles senior was a "striper," a man who paints stripes on new cars — he and his family lived a gypsy life during the Great Depression, travelling from place to place, wherever the father could find work. Settling in New York City before World War II, Miles lived in a neighborhood of Russian, Irish, and Greek immigrants, and joined an anti-Bolshevik Russian youth battalion at the age of eleven. Two years later, passing for eighteen, he joined the New York National Guard. In 1940 he graduated from high school and enlisted in DeGaulle's Free French Army. "It was all sub rosa since there was the Neutrality Act and technically you weren't supposed to enlist in foreign services," he recalled in an interview. "I liked the military concepts. I was a good radio operator when I was a child. My mother had taught French at home so I just fell into it."

"We were very disillusioned and upset by the way things had gone in Europe. France had fallen. Here the anti-Bolshevik forces of Germany supposedly had clasped the hand [in the 1939 Nazi-Soviet pact] of what to us was a Satan. We were raised to believe the power of the Bolsheviks was Satanic. That was all part of the adventure. I stayed with the Free French as a wireless operator and air gunner until the United States came into the war."

After Pearl Harbor Miles joined the U.S. Navy and fought in the South Pacific as a radio operator, later using his communications skills to handle instrument landings and underwater demolitions. He was part of the attack force in Okinawa. By the war's end Miles was in the Philippines helping a trading company set up radio operations.

After the war, Miles worked with an anti-communist Ukrainian organization, training radio operators who then went behind Soviet lines in the Ukrainian resistance. He was later employed by a British insurance company for twenty-two years, becoming a branch manager in Michigan. During the 1967 race riots in Detroit he was part of an insurance panel that dealt with riot-related insurance problems. Miles explains:

> We started to organize after the Detroit riots, and we saw Wallace as the voice who would speak for us. Since 1947 we had a discussion group called the Free Association. We were active with the Ukrainians.
>
> Mind, I was at one time the finance chairman of the Republican Party in this state. I was the editor of the *American Society of Safety Engineers Newsletter*. I was president of the Insurance Executives Society. I was an accepted member of the establishment. I wasn't stupid enough to think I could wear a white robe while I attended their meetings. I knew there was a line, and there was going to be a price to pay.
>
> So we started to work for the governor. We thought that he was going to be our hope, a third party ticket. We really thought you could build a third party in this country. We failed to realize that the only way third parties become major parties is when they split one of the two existing parties and take over one of the split parts.
>
> We went into the Wallace movement publicly. I announced to the newspapers that I was leaving the Republican Party. We started to work

Make a List of Your Enemies

[Excerpts from a Robert Miles speech made in the early 1980s to a gathering of racist youth in Detroit.]

We are going to deal with the four phases of racial resistance. Four parts: the legal political party, the racial guerrilla theater, the racial theological mission, and finally, the culmination, the racial armed party. All resistance groups, whether of the left or the right, black, white or whatever nationality, wherever they are, are composed of those four basic elements. . . .

The legal party is the political arena of struggle. I'd like to see every one of you pitting yourself against the foe, tackling one issue in your own precinct. And running. And I don't care what you run as. You can run as an independent if you choose, or a Democrat, or a Republican. In fact it would be good if there was ten of you in the county, five run as a Democrat, five run as a Republican. Then no matter who the sheep vote for, they get one of us. That's the way the left has done it. That's the way the atheists have done it. It's worked for them and it can work for us. . . . We're not bringing anyone to our side. We are only interested in you bringing out, out of the darkness those who are truly the children of light.

Be assured. Be confident. When the armed party comes it will be announced by its deeds—not by speeches, not by literature and not by any press conference at which they announce the formation of a new secret resistance. The type of press conference that the armed party will give will leave nobody to write any obituary columns at the local newspaper. It's come. You are the pathfinders. You are the teachers. Your role is to light the torches in the darkness and keep those torches lit so that when that army does come you can guide them down the path.

Every one of you has an assignment. If you didn't have it before now . . . you have it now. You are to list in your own community all those who are active friends and all those who are active foes. . . . When I ask you who is your enemy in Oshkosh, who is the enemy of your race, I don't want to hear Menachem Begin, Josef Stalin or Kubla Khan. We want to know who is working against your interests in your own backyard, by name, address, age, association, block where he is, what he looks like, who he travels with, who he goes to bed with, what he does in the morning, what he does in the afternoon, what he does in the evening. . . . You're an intelligence agency. Now get to work so when the army comes, and the knock comes on your door, and the man says give me the list, you don't say, "List? I've got a shopping list. Oh. I don't know. There are no communists around here. I don't really know."

A night will come when in the birth pains of freedom for our race the armed party is born. Your role is to prepare for that hour, you provide that information, and to get working on it right now. Three by five cards are your weapon. Newspaper clippings are your weapon. One man or ten or twenty . . . and you read your newspapers, and you put down John Silberstein on one card, and then underneath that you put down the Human Rights Activists Commission Against the Klan. Another card, you entitle that the Human Rights Activist Commission Against the Klan; you put John Silberstein. Two files, cross-indexed . . . until each of you has an intelligence file in his own home, capable of serving the army when it comes. You've got to be a guide. You've got to be a seer. And you have a feel, you have a spirit, and that spirit tells you when and where and how. . . .

The armed party comes when the federal government in this country disintegrates, and it is disintegrating right before your eyes today. In the aftermath of a three-day nuclear strike . . . The words and laws of the federal government in Washington will be like winds howling through the cesspools of the Bronx. . . .

for the election of the governor in 1968. I first became affiliated with the United Klans of America, which was under the discipline of Wallace and his precinct task force in the old days.

If you remember, in his first race for governor of Alabama, Wallace ran against "Kissing Jim" Folsom. But Kissing Jim had the support of the local Klan in Alabama. Wallace had the support of the NAACP and B'nai B'rith. They had openly come out for him, and he lost. That's when Wallace said he'd never again be "outniggered." Soon thereafter we see Bob Shelton rising. He was an automobile worker, a very capable, young ex–army sergeant. He whipped together a Klan that was comprised of all these independent Klans — like the Dixie Klan, the U.S. Klan, the Georgia Klan — and he combined them into the United Klans of America. It was loyal to Wallace. They were his precinct task force in the old days. Other than the Birchers, they were the hardest working group in the third party movement. The Birch Society was always suspect. They did not have loyalty to Wallace personally. They didn't follow a chieftain. They followed Robert Welch, the candy maker up in Massachusetts.

Tom Turnipseed, Wallace's national campaign manager, remembers Miles from the campaign:

He was kind of our main campaign person in Michigan. At the time we had a motley crew of various racists, you know, people who just had been freaked out by the civil rights movement, anti-Vietnam movement and the like. There were all kinds of folks involved in the Wallace thing. Miles was a cut above the other people, a kind of a businessman. He seemed to be more educated generally than the typical Wallace supporter. And I was very surprised later on when he went further and further out into never-never land. He told me at the time he was just a businessman and these riots just bothered him a lot . . . I always wondered about him. . . .

We tried to keep the Klan down and out of the situation generally. Wallace would try to keep

Book by Robert Miles, subtitled "A Guide To Ritual with Proposed Adaptations To Fit the Needs of the Order in the 5th Era," published in 1983, which argued for a new —underground — era in organizing.

those guys out. He didn't want them up front. His typical retort to the press when they asked him about the Klan was, "I have never been to a Klan rally and don't advocate violence," which was probably true. He walked a fine line.

Still, the Wallace campaign — and the whiff of real, honest-to-God mass politics it gave them — was very important to the racists. "We reactivated Klan ties — ties that were very remote to us then, but which became useful to us today," Miles said.

We knew we weren't going to win, but we thought we'd do [even] better than we did. We got ten million votes, which was fantastic. On election night Wallace asked us to take charge of the party — not me personally, but a loyalist group of which I was a part — and to remove the Birchers from positions of authority and replace them with Wallace loyalists, which we did. I became secretary of the party. One of the key parts to that was the use of the United Klan up here, which at the time was fairly small. But they were good southern loyalists and they were disciplined. In order to maintain control I took the Klan over myself. That's how I became grand dragon. I was elected in the summer of 1969 — I became the grand dragon and beginning in 1970 I became national chaplain.

Robert Miles, former Grand Dragon of the Michigan Ku Klux Klan and leader of the racist right, shown here (far right) during a 1971 anti-busing rally in Pontiac, Michigan.

In 1973 Miles drew a nine-year federal prison term for his role in planning the bombing of empty school buses that were to be used in a busing program in Pontiac during 1971. He was also convicted of an attack on a Willow Run, Michigan school principal, who was tarred and feathered. (Miles had pled not guilty on both charges.) He served six years of the nine-year sentence, much of it in the federal government's maximum security prison at Marion, Illinois. After prison Miles returned to his Cohoctah, Michigan farm, where he was pastor of the local Mountain Church (and became known as the "Old Man of the Mountain"). There he preached the Dualist religion, which, like Christian Identity, provides a theological underpinning to racialist politics. In Dualism, as Miles has explained it, whites were sent to earth by God to conquer it for him in a great final battle with his rebellious former crown prince, who had gathered a force of look-alike angels made of "dirt, dust, and mud."

WAR

Miles at one time oversaw the activities of fifteen different churches, and along with Richard Butler of the Aryan Nations, waged a vigorous ministry among prison inmates. He published a monthly newsletter entitled *From the Mountain*, as well as other publications, including a guidebook on how to set up a Klan chapter. The newsletter subscription list ran to 3,600 people, nearly half of them in prison — he once referred to his work as "The Salvation Army mission of the radical racial resistance." A movement newsletter described Miles's position "as a counsel and advisor to any and all racial activists and organizations. In the state of Michigan Miles has established a council that enables feuds, frictions and factionalism to be avoided. . . . The role of the Mountain Kirk [Miles's church] is that of racial theological mission to provide services and sacraments to those White Christians who no longer feel comfortable or welcome within the confines of the humanistic, judaicized, pseudo-Christian institutions. Miles is a member of the Aryan Nations and its Ambassador to Michigan."

His newsletter was filled with world news as it affected racial issues (for example, the supposed Jewish migration to Brazil), squibs about different figures in the movement, the prison odysseys of various members, bits of poetry, religious musings, and tub thumping for his favorite cause: racial separatism. In his pursuit of this cause, Miles maintained an ongoing relationship with the Aryan Nations, and was accused of receiving money from the underground's robberies. He denied it.

During the 1980s Miles's Cohoctah farm, not far from Flint, Michigan, became a meeting place for different factions of the far right, among which

"Take Off the Hoods!"
Scream Our Foes

[Excerpts from a Robert Miles letter to the September/October 1988 issue of The Klansman, *published by the Invisible Empire of the Knights of the Ku Klux Klan.]*

"Take off the hoods!", scream our foes. "Come out into the open if you are not ashamed of what you believe in!", is the cry of the liberal, the do-gooder, and the federal traitors.

What they are really saying is, "Come out and let us get a better shot at you!" And they mean just that! Well, Klansmen, let us resolve any questions or doubts which you may have about this viper-emanating hiss.

The word "Invisible" in "Invisible Empire" means just that. It describes the condition of the White Racial Resistance. It describes the manner in which that Resistance is to operate. . . . Secrecy may not be fully possible in this electronic age, but privacy, or a degree of secrecy, is quite possible. Secrecy is what bedeviled the federal tyrants during the first era of our Order, the courageous Ku Klux Klan. Secrecy is what enables the few to confuse, confound, and conquer the many. It was the ability of the stalwart bands of individuals, surrounded on all sides by congoids and Washington-based satraps and local sell-outs, to appear, to disappear, and to re-appear, that gave our South, and the White Race, its most heroic victory. . . .

The television era of the Klan, the fourth era, is dying and passing into history. It has served us well. But its age is over. Its duty has been done. We now enter the fifth era. . . .

Invisibility is a weapon. It is the characteristic of the Order. It was the reason why our Order gained political power in the first era. It does work. It can work. It shall work again.

Those who are the spokesmen, the public lecturers and the open contacts for the Klan, can't become "Invisible". They accept the limitations and the burdens which such entails. They are the lightning rods which the foes fury falls upon in times of the storm. Yet, they have the responsibility to safeguard those who are private, secret, or "invisible". Just as the lightning rod protects the ones inside the house, so must these human lightning rods and periscopes protect the ones who form the grand body of the organization. But let none confuse the roles! From here on in, the bulk of the membership MUST be secret! And that takes work. It takes planning and effort on the part of all leaders, at all levels. If the Klan is to again obtain political power, it must once again regain the use of the tool which gave it its greatest victory.

So don't let the taunts of the foe cause you to raise your head above the trenches so that he can get a better shot at you. Understand your role. Understand that we are in enemy-occupied territory and that no guerrilla force wears parade uniforms into battle. No special forces unit wears medals into combat. No covert army ever succeeded where it let the foe choose the time of battle, the territory on which to fight, nor the manner in which to fight. We are to be as the fog; as the first of God! Let us again begin to plan, and to act in deadly seriousness as we begin to train once more. For if we do not, then we shall be quite dead—literally!

Pastor Robert E. Miles,
former Grand Dragon, Realm of Michigan
for the United Klans of America,
and current head of the
Mountain Church, Cohactah, Michigan

Miles sought to promote unity. At one three-day meeting in April 1986, for example, perhaps 200 people showed up. They included such leaders as Glenn Miller of the White Patriot Party from North Carolina; Thom Robb, the Christian Identity preacher who was also national chaplain for the KKK; Debbie Mathews, widow of the martyred Order leader Bob Mathews; William Pierce, author of the *Turner Diaries*; and Don Black, the Alabama Klansman who had been imprisoned for conspiracy to invade the Caribbean island of Dominica, and who was then running for the U.S. Senate in his state's Republican primary. Representatives from Canada's racist organizations, including John Ross Taylor, head of the fascist Western Guard, also made speeches.

Participants at this gathering listened to talks on the history of the movement, tedious harangues against Jews, blacks, and other "mud people," and even a report on Satanic ritual murders. Events culminated in a cross burning on the back lot of the farm. Garbed in a Scottish kilt Miles held forth, acting as master of ceremonies and officiating as minister at a Klan marriage conducted by flashlight under the smoldering cross. He was also an indomitable advocate of an out-trek to the Pacific Northwest, where Aryans could set up an all-white homeland. Throughout, Miles did his best to broker competition among different groups, sternly advising everyone not to carry firearms, and warning the gathering to take care that their cars weren't pockmarked by the fire from the cross burning, and to beware of the press.

Off the Beam

In his efforts to pull together the divergent strands of the white resistance movement, Bob Miles had joined with Louis R. Beam, Jr., also an ambassador to the Aryan Nations, in editing a short-lived publication called the *Inter-klan Newsletter and Survival Alert*. Beam, a former helicopter gunner in Vietnam, was another member of the David Duke generation; in the late 1970s he had been the grand dragon of David Duke's Texas Knights of the Ku Klux Klan. Beam was one of the Aryan Nations' most zealous and bloodcurdling members, a vocally uncompromising enthusiast who loudly declared his intention to personally wring the neck of China's then–deputy premier Deng Xiaoping on his visit to the U.S. in 1976. He was also the reputed mastermind of the Aryan Nations' computer network and assassination hit list. Beam's motto was, "Where ballots fail, bullets will prevail."

The *Inter-klan Newsletter and Survival Alert* provided a forum for the often squabbling groups on the far right, and set out a general vision of the next phase of the Klan — what it called the Fifth Era Klan. Both Miles and Beam saw the Klans and other rightist groups as part of a political movement. But Miles was considerably more ecumenical than his colleague, seeing the need for many different forms of action — ranging from participation in political activities and cultural and social organizations to a vigorous underground. He argued for harnessing the survivalist movement into a trek to a new Aryan homeland (a la the Confederate Knights of the Golden Circle), and he encouraged both Glenn Miller's pursuit of a Senate seat in North Carolina and Don Black's candidacy in Alabama. Beam, on the other hand, was a mad dog, yearning for the pounding hooves of the night riders and the old-fashioned justice of the noose. For him the underground was everything. The *Inter-klan Newsletter* put it this way:

This country is moving irresistibly toward internal armed conflict between those who fight for their heritage and those who seek to destroy it. The enemy has managed to capture the government. So, for the third time in this nation's history, the government has become the enemy of the people. The first time this occurred [under British colonial rule], our nation was able to produce resolute intelligent leaders, who directed the American people in a war against the government. Death, violence, suffering, and sacrifice ruled supreme for seven long years, but eventually the people won — the government overthrown and the Republic born.

Many years later during Reconstruction, a hate-filled and vindictive government violated its own terms of surrender given to a valiant but defeated foe who had sought independence. An attempt was made to enslave the people of the South — at the hands of their former slaves. Once again the people were led by great leaders to fight the government, and where open combat had failed, secret struggle was successful. So shall it be in the Fifth Era, for the Anglo-Saxon does not long bow to the heavy hand of tyranny.

"We do not advocate . . . segregation," the *Inter-klan Newsletter and Survival Alert* argued. "That was a temporary political measure and that time is past." Instead, "the Greater White Racialist Movement intends to establish for our White Aryan Race what every other Race on Earth has: A racial homeland. . . . Our Order intends to take part in the Physical and Spiritual Racial Purification of ALL those countries which have traditionally been considered White Lands in Modern Times. . . . We intend to purge this land-area of Every Non-White person, idea and influence . . . IN SUMMARY: This continent will be white or it will not be at all. . . ."

"The vast majority of the White Race will continue to oppose the Klan and any other racial movement," the newsletter said. "It is . . . pure fantasy to imagine the Klan as a broad-based movement that will . . . effect peaceful change. . . .

There should be no doubt that all means short of armed conflict have been exhausted."

Beam created a point system for evaluating the relative worth of different targets for the underground, giving the most points to killing influential individuals rather than to raining indiscriminate terror down on blacks and other minorities, as had been common practice among the Ku Klux Klans. As the newsletter proclaimed:

We of America's racial right, along with white-men of our persuasion everywhere, want to be alive to hunt down and punish the bastards who put us in this plight in the first place.

One by one, two by two, or fifteen at a time we want them — all of them — every last filthy money-grubbing politician, lawyer, judge, law-breaking government agent, media mongrel, lying preacher, and race traitor. . . . The human scum . . . to be hunted down like the mad, rabid dogs they are. Praise God! The day of the wolf will have arrived. We strike in surrogate for all the children bused to black ghettos and brutalized, for all the little girls dragged from the parks and raped, for all the families murdered while they slept, for all the young men sent to die in no-win wars in forgotten lands for unknown causes and for all the unspeakable heinous crimes unleashed upon civilized society. My tow-sack runneth over with the heads of enemies.

In the late 1980s, both Miles and Beam were charged with being at the center of a secret seditious conspiracy to plot violent strikes against the government, engaging in robberies and counterfeiting, bombing utility pipelines and electrical transmission lines, plotting robberies against Jewish targets, and conspiring in the deaths of an FBI agent and a federal judge. They were acquitted at a jury trial in Fort Smith, Arkansas in 1989. By that time, Miles's semiannual leadership gatherings at his farm had ceased. Tired of his long fights with the feds, and with his wife seriously ill, Miles finally put his Flint farm up for sale. Beam's computerized hit list was a thing of the past, too, but in 1990, the fiery chopper gunner continued to be the hottest spark on the far right's lecture circuit.

The Aryan Nations and the Order

While Bob Miles's involvement in the Wallace presidential bid impressed white revolutionaries with the potential power of an above-ground political movement, Beam's example kept alive the tradition of clandestine terror. But the violent white supremacist underground surfaced in earnest for the first time in 1983 in a stunning series of robberies, murders, and shootouts with western state police. The press gave this shadowy movement various names: the Order, the White American Bastion, Bruders Schweiden, the Silent Brotherhood.

The Order was in fact an underground splinter of the Aryan Nations, the organization which provided an umbrella for a network of Klans and other far-right fringe groups from its headquarters in Hayden Lake, Idaho. The Aryan Nations traces its origins back through sixty years of far-right history: As Kevin Flynn and Gary Gerhardt recount in *The Silent Brotherhood*, the Aryan Nations' leader, Richard Butler, had been introduced to the racialist movement at the California Christian Identity Church of Wesley Swift, the former aide to Gerald L.K. Smith. At Swift's church Butler had also met William Gale, who later became a major figure in the Posse Comitatus. Upon Swift's death, Butler took over his church, eventually moving it to Hayden Lake, Idaho, and making it a part of the Aryan Nations movement. In the 1960s Butler set

Aryan Nations Oath of Allegiance

"I, as a free Aryan man, hereby swear an unrelenting oath upon the green graves of our sires, upon the children in the wombs of our wives, upon the throne of God almighty, sacred is His name, to join together in holy union with those brothers in this circle and to declare forthright that from this moment on I have no fear of death, no fear of foe; that I have a sacred duty to do whatever is necessary to deliver our people from the Jew and bring total victory to the Aryan race.

"I, as an Aryan warrior, swear myself to complete secrecy to the Order and total loyalty to my comrades.

"Let me bear witness to you, my brothers, that should one of you fall in battle, I will see to the welfare and well-being of your family.

"Let me bear witness to you, my brothers, that should one of you be taken prisoner, I will do whatever is necessary to regain your freedom.

"Let me bear witness to you my brothers, that should an enemy agent hurt you, I will chase him to the ends of the earth and remove his head from his body.

"And furthermore, let me bear witness to you, my brothers, that if I break this oath, let me be forever cursed upon the lips of our people as a coward and an oath breaker.

"My brothers let us be His battle ax and weapons of war. Let us go forth by ones and twos, by scores and by legions, and as true Aryan men with pure hearts and strong minds face the enemies of our faith and our race with courage and determination.

"We hereby invoke the blood covenant and declare that we are in a full state of war and will not lay down our weapons until we have driven the enemy into the sea and reclaimed the land which was promised of our fathers of old, and through our blood and His will, becomes the land of our children to be."

The DEATH of the WHITE RACE

U.S. COMMISSIONER CONFIRMS THAT WHITE PEOPLE FACE EXTINCTION.

For years Aryan Nations has been warning our White kin that there was a conspiracy to Murder our White Aryan Race and that we were fast approaching the point of no return.

Now we have confirmation from U. S. Government sources. On the back of this leaflet you will find a reproduction of an article from the August 4, 1981, Rocky Mountain News. When reading the article, please bear in mind the following things.

Considering the lower-than-replacement White birth rate, the high non-white birthrate, the colored immigration, and the fact that thousands of our young people (especially our women) desert their Race every day to marry non-whites, you can see that in ten years the child-bearing population of America will be less than ten percent White.

All history, as well as common sense, declares that no Race can survive without separation from others so they can promote, propagate, and protect their own kind.

THE ULTIMATE ABOMINATION

There are over two dozen all-Black nations engaging in no integration or the inevitable resultant, miscegenation, which decrees the death of a Race. The population of one Yellow country alone, China, is nearly four times all the Whites on the Planet. They, too, are remaining racially pure. There are no all-White nations, at least in the Western world. We are the earth's most endangered species.

The famous American aviator, Charles Lindberg, travelled America in the 30's warning that if we helped to destroy the tiny nation of Germany, which was the last and only White Racial Nation, then our Race was doomed. Was he right?

Today YOU can escape the terror of the Black ghettos and the Brown barrios. Your children and your children's children will have no refuge. The DEATH OF THE WHITE RACE is neither imaginary nor far off in the distant future. History shows what "tender mercy" the few remaining Whites can expect from the colored hordes in the last days of our Race.

The JEWS, who have sworn to destroy our Race and who now own all three T.V. networks, the major movie companies, and nearly all newspapers and publishing companies, make it front page headlines, if they can find a non-integrated school or neighborhood anywhere.

Nations, economic systems, political systems, etc., will rise, fall, and evolve as long as man walks this planet. The DEATH OF THE WHITE RACE is eternal. Make no mistake, WHITEMAN, the death of our Race, the creators of Law, Justice, Technology, Medicine, Housing - virtually everything of value - spells the end of civilization.

Whiteman, look at the beautiful woman you love. Whitewoman, think about the future for your children. WHITEMAN, THINK. The decision is for this generation. Your children will be outnumbered fifty to one by colored people, who have been inflamed to hatred of our people by the JEWSMEDIA. Nature's laws are as impartial as they are harsh. Love your own kind, fight for your own kind or perish, as have many thousands of other species.

YOUR FIRST LOYALTY MUST BE TO YOUR RACE WHICH IS YOUR NATION !

Make copies of this leaflet and give them to everyone you know. Our Race is nearly out of time. For more information write to: Aryan Nations, P.O. Box362, Hayden Lake, Idaho 83835.

ARYAN NATIONS

Flyer distributed by the Aryan Nations in 1981.

up a twenty-acre compound with about 100 residents, equipped with a church-school and a paramilitary training ground. Hayden Lake became a Mecca for adherents of the far right, who moved to the upper Northwest and paid regular visits to the compound.

The Aryan Nations ideology is saturated with Christian Identity teachings, and Butler himself was a pastor of the Christian Identity Church of Jesus Christ Christian. Butler recruited in penitentiaries through the Aryan Brotherhood, a white supremacist prison gang whose motto was the tattoo-perfect: "Kill to get in. Die to get out."

In 1982, the Aryan Nations staged the first International Congress of Aryan Nations. Hayden Lake became a gathering point, a sort of communal campfire of the right where one could learn about far-right history, politics, and culture. Among the major drawing points was a book called *Turner Diaries* by William Pierce, the former Oregon State University physics professor who had been a publicist for George Lincoln Rockwell's American Nazi Party, then an editor for the World Union of National Socialists. In 1968 Pierce had joined Willis Carto's Youth for Wallace, and later founded its offshoot, the National Alliance, which carried forward the defense of a white world. *Turner Diaries* is the story of a right-wing white revolution, and of an underground group called the Order, which spearheads the rebellion. Long before the real-life Order had made its name in the press as the violent underground terrorist force of the far right, *Turner Diaries* had achieved cult status, being traded at book stalls at far-right meetings and sold through movement fanzines, as well as through gun and survivalist magazines. It became the movement's Bible.

Among the up-and-coming young leaders at the Alliance was a personable lumberjack named Bob Mathews, who lived in Metaline Falls, Washington. Mathews had grown up outside Phoenix during the early 1960s in an atmosphere defined by Goldwater's 1964 presidential campaign. As a young man Mathews joined the John Birch Society, trained with a survivalist-style group called the Sons of Liberty, and became active in the tax protest movement. Later he joined the National Alliance. He was arrested for tax fraud and put on probation. On a trip through the Northwest he fell in love with Washington, and soon resettled his whole family in the state. Not long after, he announced that he had found the perfect church for white people, a three-hour drive away at Hayden Lake, Idaho. It was called the Church of Jesus Christ Christian.

Mathews knew the men who coalesced around the Aryan Nations compound, and he offered one of them, Bruce Carroll Pierce (no relation to William), a job cutting timber on his property. After he had been working there a while, Mathews asked Pierce whether he would be interested in forming a group like the "Order" depicted in *Turner Diaries*. Soon a group of eight men were meeting formally to discuss the concept of the new Order. In the beginning the goals were loosely defined, but everyone agreed the new organization would fight for a territorial imperative that defined the northwestern United States as "the last bastion of white predominance," and called for its formal secession.

In a statement taken down by the FBI (and later recanted), Bruce Pierce said that he "hoped for a natural disaster, economic failure of the U.S. government, a major race war, or anything that would disrupt society in America so that he would be able to gather up his army of men and strike against the system, that being the U.S. government. Bob Mathews's intent was to destroy those instruments standing in the way of Aryans having

Aryan Nations founder Richard Butler stands under a stained glass symbol of his group in his Hayden Lake, Idaho church in 1985.

a homeland for the white race. All other members of the organization fell in line behind Mathews and followed like sheep."

At first the members of the group decided to fund the operations of their new organization through legitimate means, and they bid on what looked to be a profitable trail-clearing contract with the U.S. Forest Service. But the work was hard, and took more time than expected. When it started to snow, Mathews persuaded the rest to abandon it. He then proposed to raise money for the Order by means of armed robberies, and everyone agreed.

In April of 1983, fund-raising for the "war chest" got going in a serious way when three members of the Order walked into a Spokane porn shop. While one of them distracted the clerk at the cash register, another slugged a second clerk in the mouth. The three revolutionaries fled with a take of $369. Next they scouted Seattle for a good site to stage an armored car robbery, but abandoned that temporarily in favor of counterfeiting fifty-dollar bills on the Aryan Nations printing press at Hayden Lake. But they had a hard time getting the color right, and when they tried to pass the money in Yakima, Washington, Bruce Pierce was arrested. He was held for about a month, then released on bond, and immediately fled. In December 1983, Bob Mathews walked into a Seattle branch of Citibank, handed the teller a note, and walked out with $25,900.

The tempo of robberies picked up speed. In March of 1984, members of the Order successfully made off with $43,000 from an armored car parked outside a Fred Meyers store in Seattle. They ambushed the courier, took the money, and ran. Next the Order hit another armored car at a Seattle Bon Marche outlet, making off with $500,000. From this money they made a $40,000 contribution to the Aryan Nations church, and discussed

making contributions elsewhere. A few days after the Bon Marche robbery Bruce Pierce put a bomb under a Boise synagogue, but it caused little damage. In the spring of 1984, the group returned to counterfeiting, this time enlisting the aid of an old-time, accomplished counterfeiter, and they began turning out money that looked real enough.

Meanwhile, there were internal squabbles. When Walter West, one of the men on the fringes of the Order, was thought to be talking too much, the others grew nervous that they would be found out. West was lured into a car and driven to a spot a couple of hours outside Boise, where a group from the Order were waiting. When West got out of the car, someone hit him on the head with a sledgehammer; when the hammer blow didn't kill him, another member shot him through the forehead with a Mini-14 semiautomatic rifle. The men buried the body in the wilderness, and one of them later moved in with West's wife.

To further their goal of killing all their enemies, the Order's leaders now set out to murder

Turner Diaries

[Written in 1978 by William Pierce, Turner Diaries *helped launch the Order, the covert military arm of the Aryan Nations. This futuristic book describes a group of whites who start an all-out race war for the "Great Revolution," thus establishing white supremacy in the United States.]*

August 1, 1993. Today has been the Day of the Rope—a grim and bloody day, but an unavoidable one. Tonight, for the first time in weeks, it is quiet and totally peaceful throughout all of southern California. But the night is filled with silent horrors; from tens of thousands of lampposts, power poles, and trees throughout this vast metropolitan area the grisly forms hang.

THE TURNER DIARIES

Andrew Macdonald

In the lighted areas one sees them everywhere. Even the street signs at intersections have been pressed into service, and at practically every street corner I passed this evening on my way to HQ there was a dangling corpse, four at every intersection. Hanging from a single overpass only about a mile from here is a group of about 30, each with an identical placard around its neck bearing the printed legend, "I betrayed my race." Two or three of that group had been decked out in academic robes before they were strung up, and the whole batch are apparently faculty members from the nearby UCLA campus.

In the areas to which we have not yet restored electrical power the corpses are less visible, but the feeling of horror in the air there is even worse than in the lighted areas. I had to walk through a two-block-long, unlighted residential section between HQ and my living quarters after our unit meeting tonight. In the middle of one of the unlighted blocks I saw what appeared to be a person standing on the sidewalk directly in front of me. As I approached the silent figure, whose features were hidden in the shadow of a large tree overhanging the sidewalk, it remained motionless, blocking my way.

Feeling some apprehension, I slipped my pistol out of its holster. Then, when I was within a dozen feet of the figure, which had been facing away from me, it began turning slowly toward me. There was something indescribably eerie about the movement, and I stopped in my tracks as the figure continued to turn. A slight breeze rustled the foliage overhead, and suddenly a beam of moonlight broke through the leaves and fell directly on the silently turning shape before me.

The first thing I saw in the moonlight was the placard with its legend in large, block letters: "I defiled my race." Above the placard leered the horribly bloated, purplish face of a young woman, her eyes wide open and bulging, her mouth agape. Finally I could make out the thin, vertical line of rope disappearing into the branches above. Apparently the rope had slipped a bit or the branch to which it was tied had sagged, until the woman's feet were resting on the pavement, giving the uncanny appearance of a corpse standing upright of its own volition.

I shuddered and quickly went on my way. There are many thousands of hanging female corpses like that in this city tonight, all wearing identical placards around their necks. They are the White women who were married to or living with Blacks, with Jews, or with other non-white males.

National Alliance founder and Turner Diaries *author William Pierce as he attended a gathering of white racists at Bob Miles's Michigan farm in 1986.*

Alan Berg, the controversial, Jewish host of a Denver radio talk show, who had argued on the air — pretty successfully, by all accounts — with members of the Order who had phoned in. On June 18, 1984, several Order leaders followed Berg home from work, waited for him to get out of his car, and then machine-gunned him to death.

Expenses continued to mount. The group dispatched one of their number to Philadelphia to pass the counterfeit money. They surveyed Boise in hopes of setting up another armored car heist, but police vigilance discouraged them. Instead, they laid out plans for a robbery in California, where they found willing supporters in two Brinks employees. One of these employees described a place along the armored car's route that he thought made for a natural holdup spot: a deserted country road outside Ukiah, in the California redwoods far north of San Francisco. There, on July 19, 1984, the Order staged a holdup that had all the earmarks of a paramilitary raid.

Using two pickup trucks, the members of the Order forced the armored car off the road. Twelve men piled out of the trucks and demanded that the driver and guards get out. When nothing happened, one of the men sprayed the windshield with automatic-rifle fire. At that, the driver and guards opened the door and jumped down, but a woman guard in the rear compartment — where the money was kept — refused to get out. The white revolutionaries blasted out the truck tires, then strafed the side windows. Finally the woman got out, and the Order men formed a human chain to transfer $3.6 million into the pickups. After splitting up, they met back in Boise to divide the money.

Some of the money from the Ukiah heist went to salaries, mobile homes, and even a ski condo. The group bought 110 acres in Idaho for a paramilitary training camp, and 160 acres in Missouri for another training site. They purchased uniforms and gear, including all-terrain vehicles and plenty of guns and ammo. One man was hired to provide military training. Two men formed a corporation called Mountain Man Supply Company for the sole purpose of equipping the Order. Most members quit their day jobs. And there was

Bob Mathews' Last Letter

[In December of 1984, shortly before he was killed in a shootout with the FBI, Order leader Robert Mathews wrote this letter.]

For the past decade I have been a resident of Northern Pend Oreille County. When I first arrived in Metaline Falls I had only twenty-five dollars to my name, a desire to work hard and be left alone, and the dream of someday acquiring my own small farm.

During my three years at the mine and seven years at the cement plant I can safely say that I was known as a hard worker. I stayed out of the bars and pretty much kept to myself. Anyone who is familiar with Boundary Dam Road knows how my late father and I carved a beautiful place out of the woods. All of the goals I had when I arrived were accomplished but one. . . . I was not left alone.

Within months of my arrival the FBI went to the mine office and tried to have me fired from my job. I was working in the electrical department at the time and my foreman, fortuately, had a deep and lasting dislike for the Feds. He was informed of the situation by the mine secretary. Had it been the mine manager instead of the secretary that the Government goons talked to, I would have lost my job.

This campaign of harrassment and intimidation began because of my involvement in the Tax-Rebellion Movement from the time I was fifteen to twenty years old. The Government was on me so much in Arizona that during one incident when I was eighteen, IRS agents shot at me for nothing more than a misdemeanor tax violation.

I left Arizona and the Tax-Rebellion when I was twenty. I left not out of fear of the IRS or because of submission to their tyranny, but because I was thoroughly disgusted with the American people. I maintained then as I do now, that our people have devolved into some of the most cowardly, sheepish, degenerates that have ever littered the face of this planet.

I had hoped to start a new life in the state of Washington, but the ruling powers had other plans for me. When I learned of their highly illegal attempt to have me fired, I wrote a letter to their Seattle office and told them "I would take no more, to leave me alone, or I would respond in such a way that could be very painful to certain agents." After the letter they gradually started to let me be.

I soon settled down to marriage, clearing my land, and reading. Reading became an obsession with me. I consumed volume upon volume on subjects dealing with history, politics, and economics. I was especially taken with Spengler's "Decline of the West". . . .

By the time my son had arrived I realized that White America, indeed my entire race, was headed for oblivion unless white men rose and turned the tide. The more I came to love my son the more I realized that unless things changed radically, by the time he was my age, he would be a stranger in his own land, a blond-haired, blue eyed Aryan in a country populated mainly by mexicans, mulattoes, blacks and asians. His future was growing darker by the day.

I came to learn that this was not by accident, that there is a small, cohesive alien group within this nation working day and night to make this happen. I learned that these culture distorters have an iron grip on both major political parties, on Congress, on the media, on the publishing houses, and on most of the major christian denominations in this nation, even though these aliens subscribe to a religion which is diametrically opposed to christianity. . . . Thus I have no choice. I must stand up like a white man and do battle.

A secret war has been developing for the last year between the regime in Washington and an ever growing number of white people who are determined to regain what *our* forefathers discovered, explored, conquered, settled, built, and died for.

The FBI has been able to keep this war secret only because up until now we have been doing nothing more then growing and preparing. The government, however, seems determined to force the issue, so we have no choice left but to stand up and fight back. Hail Victory!

It is at this point that I wish to address the multitude of lies that the federals have been telling about Gary Lee Yarbrough and myself. . . .

The incompetence of these gun toting bureaucrats never ceases to amaze me. Especially after their attempted ambush and murder of myself in a Portland motel. First, let me say that the FBI was not there to arrest Gary but to ambush me. They didn't even know that Gary was in the room. The only reason they were able to find me was because a trusted friend in room 14 was actually a traitor and an informant. The FBI has vast resources and the latest technology but the quality of their agents is going down hill with evey new recruit. That's because most of the best white men in this country are starting to realize that to be an FBI agent is to be nothing more than a mercenary, for the ADL and Tel Aviv.

When I stepped out of my motel room that morning, a gang of armed men came running at me. None of the men had uniforms on and the only thing they said was "stop, you bastard". At this, I yelled to Gary who was still inside and I leaped down the stairwell and took off running into the parking lot. A women agent shot at my back and the bullet missed and hit the motel manager. I rounded the corner of the motel and took off down the hill into a residential area. After running for two blocks I decided to quit being the hunted and become the hunter. I drew my gun and waited behind a concrete wall for the agents to draw near. When I aimed my gun at the head of the closest agent I saw the handsome face of a young white man and lowered my aim to his knee and his foot. Had I not done so I could have killed both agents and still had left the use of my hand which is now mangled beyond repair and which I might very well lose altogether. That is the last time I will ever give quarter.

As for the traitor in room 14, we will eventually find him. If it takes ten years and we have to travel to the far ends of the earth we will find him. And true to our oath when we do find him, we will remove his head from his body.

I have no regrets or apologies to make for Gary or myself. In fact I am proud that we had the courage and the determination to stand up and fight for our race and our heritage at a time in our history when such a deed is called a crime and not an act of valor.

Approximately nine months ago the FBI went to my house while I was away and threatened my two year old son. That was a very big mistake on their part. After the Portland shootout they went to my house and threatened my sixty-three year old mother. Such brave men they are.

I am not going into hiding, rather I will press the FBI and let them know what it is like to become the hunted. Doing so it is only logical to assume that my days on this planet are rapidly drawing to a close. Even so, I have no fear. For the reality of life is death, and the worst the enemy can do to me is shorten my tour of duty in this world. I will leave knowing that my family and friends love me and support me. I will leave knowing I have made the ultimate sacrifice to secure the future of my children.

As always, for blood, soil, honor, for faith and for race.

Robert Jay Mathews

UPI/BETTMANN NEWSPHOTOS
Order leader Robert Mathews attends an Aryan Nations rally in Spokane, Washington in 1983 — a year and a half before he is killed by an FBI SWAT team.

discussion of making contributions to Bob Miles, Glenn Miller, the Aryan Nations, and William Pierce of the National Alliance. The future looked bright for white revolution.

But in the confusion of the Ukiah robbery, Bob Mathews had left behind a pistol. The FBI found the gun and traced it to a Montana mailbox registered to Andrew Barnhill, a member of the Order. In the mailbox, the federal agents discovered literature from the Aryan Nations. Meanwhile, working backwards from the discarded escape vehicles, the FBI found the original owners, pieced together descriptions of the men who had bought the vehicles, and traced them to a motel in Santa Rosa, California. A check of nearby pay phones turned up calls to women in Colorado and Idaho who turned out to be Order girlfriends.

In June 1984 a man named Tom Martinez was arrested in Philadelphia by Secret Service agents when he attempted to pass counterfeit money given him by David Lane of the Order. Martinez had been involved in the racialist movement since the mid-1970s, joining the Klan in 1976 and the National Alliance in 1980. While active in the National Alliance he had met Bob Mathews and other members of the Order. As part of a plea bargain after his arrest, Martinez became a government informant. On the FBI's instructions, Martinez flew to Portland in November to meet Mathews to discuss his joining the Order and going underground. The idea was for Martinez to join a murder cell committed to killing Morris Dees, the Alabama civil rights attorney who, next to Berg, was the man most hated by the Order.

When Mathews picked up Martinez at the Portland airport, he thought he spotted the FBI surveillance and, ready for a shootout then and there, pulled out a pistol. Nothing happened and, calming down, Mathews put his gun away. Pulling away from the airport, however, Mathews again grew suspicious when a car started following them. Gary Yarborough, another Order member who was in the back seat, fixed a silencer to a MAC-10 machine gun and readied a grenade. Again nothing happened. That night at a Portland motel, Martinez managed to get away and make contact with the FBI. The next morning the feds raided the motel. Yarborough was arrested, but Mathews got away, wounding an agent in the process. He was then traced to Whidbey Island in Washington State, and eventually killed on December 8, 1984, in a thirty-six-hour shootout with the FBI.

The Portland fiasco got the FBI moving, and a far wider manhunt was organized to track down the remaining members of the Order. Twenty-four Order loyalists were ultimately arrested and charged with sixty-seven different counts of racketeering, which included conspiring in robbery, counterfeiting, and murder. By the time the case went to trial in September 1985 in Seattle federal court, thirteen had pled guilty. Ten were subsequently convicted and sentenced to substantial jail time. Another Order member, David Tate, was caught in Missouri, where he was convicted for murdering a state trooper. He got life without parole.

The Order trial brought an end to the most audacious manifestation of the white revolutionary

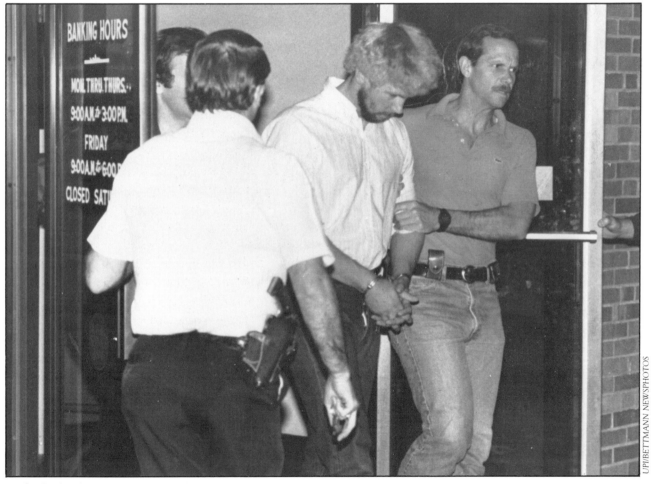

Order leader Bruce Pierce being taken into custody in 1985 in Rossville, Georgia, for questioning in the murder of Denver talk show host Alan Berg.

underground; but the Aryan Nations had provided only one highly publicized center around which the networks of the far right could coalesce. It was not the end of the movement by any means.

Glenn Miller's White Patriots

The squashing of the Order in the Northwest seemed to make the far right spurt up some 3,000 miles away, in North Carolina, where Glenn Miller and the North Carolina Knights of the Ku Klux Klan — who also called themselves the White Patriot Party — were plunging headlong into the Fifth Era.

A former Green Beret who had served two hitches in Vietnam, Miller had been a member of the American Nazi Party before 1980, then turned his energies to the Ku Klux Klan. He was in the caravan of Klan vehicles at the Greensboro massacre on November 3, 1979, when the KKK opened fire on a civil rights march. After the Greensboro killings, he changed the name of his Klan to the White Patriot Party, and by 1985, Miller claimed the party had 2,500 members and offices in six southern states. In 1984, Miller ran for governor of North Carolina and won 5,000 votes. Rebounding from that showing, in 1985 he declared himself a candidate for retiring Republican John East's Senate seat. The rally where he declared his nomination for the Senate broke up into a small arms training session.

Like many of the Fifth Era Klan factions, Miller's White Patriot Party delighted in the trappings of a military unit, wearing camouflage fatigues, emblems, and black berets. Miller was a big believer in paramilitary training camps, and there were reports that the White Patriots counted among their members Marines stationed at the Camp Lejeune training base in North Carolina. The party sponsored recorded telephone messages that could be dialed in at least fifteen locations within the state, some featuring the simulated voice of a black man being lynched.

Miller strongly supported South African apartheid. He attacked Jerry Falwell as a "Judas Goat," saying that under the guise of supporting white South Africa, the fundamentalist preacher is actually "trying to lead that country into slow, but eventual black rule." Miller also bashed Falwell for his support of Israel. By the late 1980s the White Patriot Party's phone messages had become vintage Christian Identity tracts, linking the farm depression in North Carolina to international Jewish bankers.

Miller himself said he was "ultra right plus a

million miles." The main platform of his party, he said, is "Southern independence. The creation of an all-white nation within the one million square miles of mother Dixie. We have no hope for Jew York City or San Fran-sissy-co and other areas that are dominated by Jews, perverts, and communists and non-white minorities and rectum-loving queers."

Miller was subpoenaed before the Seattle grand jury that had handed down the Order indictments in 1984. In his statement to the FBI after his arrest, Bruce Carroll Pierce had said that the Order gave Miller $300,000 from its robbery booty. Miller denied ever receiving any of the money. But after the end of 1984, Miller's activities showed a re-markable new life. That summer, during the trial, he had pleaded indigence and asked for a court-

Glenn Miller, leader of the North Carolina Knights of the Ku Klux Klan (later the White Patriot Party), being interviewed at a demonstration in Smithfield, North Carolina in 1984.

appointed attorney, claiming he lived off an $11,000-a-year Green Beret pension. But by January 1985, he had 325 Klansmen marching in Raleigh — six times more than had assembled at the capital at any time over the past five years. They had snappy new uniforms and new Confederate flags, and came equipped with video equipment, headphones, and other sophisticated communications gear.

In denying receipt of any money from the Order, Miller said, "We expect that they're [the FBI] going to frame us, plant drugs and illegal weapons on our property, pull all kinds of dirty tricks on us." As for the Aryan Nations, he said, "We exchange literature. The fact is, we practice solidarity, spiritual solidarity. And we're racial brothers and sisters, struggling for the survival of the white race."

Standing Up to the Klan

After Alan Berg, the radio talk show host riddled by Order machine-gun fire, the top man on the underground's hit list was Montgomery, Alabama attorney Morris Dees. Even as the FBI was carrying out its successful obliteration of the Order in the Northwest, other elements of the far-right underground began a methodical campaign to destroy the "Jew Morris Dees."

Dees has long been a controversial figure. An entrepreneur, he started a chicken farm as a teenager, and later organized a direct-mail birthday cake business at the University of Alabama. He actually managed to make a million dollars selling encyclopedias, and financed George McGovern's 1972 presidential bid with a direct-mail drive that produced $24 million. It was the first time direct mail had been used on such a large scale in a political campaign; Dees was an early practitioner

of what has become one of the most powerful fund-raising techniques in politics and an integral part of the 1980s political culture. He went on to become Jimmy Carter's campaign finance director, and then helped organize the campaign to draft Ted Kennedy for the 1980 Democratic presidential nomination. In 1984 he raised money for Gary Hart. All in all, one-time chicken farmer Morris Dees had established himself as one of the hottest political consultants in the Democratic Party.

But that was not why the Aryan Nations set out to murder him. As Dees rose through the technical ranks of the party, he was also busily earning a reputation as a flamboyant and aggressive civil rights advocate in Alabama. In 1971 Dees, along with Montgomery attorney Joe Levin and former Georgia state senator and civil rights leader Julian Bond, helped to found the Southern Poverty Law Center. The Center was dedicated to advancing the legal rights of the poor through education and litigation, and over the last two decades its suits have been instrumental in opening municipal and state jobs to blacks and women. It fought the death penalty, sought to block forced legal sterilization of young black women, and won improvements in prison conditions. And the Center's "Klanwatch" project, which puts out a widely circulated newsletter, has brought to light the full extent of the Klan's resurgence in recent years.

During a 1981 Klanwatch effort to help Vietnamese shrimpers in Texas who were being terrorized by armed Klansmen, Dees first encountered Louis Beam, then the grand dragon of the state's KKK. Under Beam, the rather listless Lone Star Klan had been reinvigorated. He had formed paramilitary units that trained at five different hidden camps; they happily looked forward to the day when Beam's white army would lead Texas into secession from the union.

"I'd never heard of Beam," Dees later recalled. "He followed us in a car, pointed mock guns at us. They'd follow us to our motel, call us in the middle of the night. During the trial I filed a motion to give Beam a psychiatric examination and asked the judge to put him under a protective order because he threatened to kill us."

Beam referred to Houston federal district court Judge Gabrielle McDonald as "this Negress masquerading as a federal judge." By the time the harassment trial was over, McDonald had issued an injunction ordering Beam and his Klan to leave the Vietnamese people alone. Later, the courts enjoined the Klan from paramilitary operations as well. Dees clearly had a powerful effect on Beam — after the trial, the Christian gentleman and Vietnam vet sent the lawyer and Democratic Party counselor a letter challenging him to a dual to the death. And in his 1983 *Essays of a Klansman*, Beam wrote:

> *Klanwatch*, which is published by the Jew Morris "anti-Christ" Dees (a former embezzler turned confidence man), is the official oracle of Dees' (latest in a series) of cons known as the Southern Poverty Law Center. . . . Dees has become a multi-millionaire at the expense of low-income ignorant blacks. . . . This hate sheet [*Klanwatch*] complains that "dangerous alliances are being formed between the Aryan Nations, the Canadian Klan, and the Texas Klan of Louis Beam.
>
> Yes, "dangerous," the swine says. Dangerous to whom? and why? the inquiring mind must ask. Dangerous to the parasitical Jews who steal from us, the non-whites who live off us, the government that oppresses and destroys us, and the whites who betray us. . . .

In July 1983, someone broke into the Southern Poverty Law Center building in Montgomery, sprayed gasoline over the furniture and files, and set it afire. After a seventeen-month-long investi-

gation, three local Klansmen were indicted for arson. They pleaded guilty and were sentenced to up to fifteen years in prison. One of the three also admitted to staking out Dees's house.

Then, in the summer of 1984, Beam suddenly appeared in Montgomery posing as a filmmaker taking footage of the Law Center and its staff, Dees's home, and other points of interest. Dees and his associates discovered that the filmmaker's trunk was loaded not only with film, but with rifles as well.

In December 1984, Glenn Miller announced a tie-in of White Patriot Party computers to Beam's Aryan Nations computer network. It was on that network that Dees was formally targeted for assassination. But Dees continued to gnaw away at Miller through legal channels. Just before the 1984 presidential election Dees, the Southern Poverty Law Center staff, and their guards flew to Raleigh, North Carolina, to take depositions — including Miller's — in a case Klanwatch had brought on behalf of a black prison guard who had tried to get a promotion. Klanwatch sought an injunction against the paramilitary operations of Glenn Miller's Carolina Knights of the Ku Klux Klan, who had threatened to kill the guard.

Since there was no space available at the federal courthouse, Dees arranged for a room in the Wake County courthouse, also in downtown Raleigh. "We knew they were watching the courthouse," Dees said. "We had our guards with us. But we [were in] a bad position, because the sheriff's office wouldn't help us. They wanted to stay neutral. They looked at us as some kind of left-wing communist crazy crowd, which we are not. They wanted to keep hands off us because of all that Greensboro stuff. They wouldn't let our guards carry weapons. We had to stash them in the trunk of the car."

So, as the sheriff's deputies stood by, twenty-five to thirty Klansmen, wearing camouflaged fatigues and marching in military lockstep, lined up outside the room where Dees was to take Glenn Miller's deposition.

"I went out to call Miller, the first witness," Randall Williams, then the director of Klanwatch, recalled. "All of a sudden I see this blur coming at me at a pretty good clip across the room. I wheel around and this guy is right there coming at me. . . . He had a camera. He got right in my face and was still coming. I put my hand up and the camera came right into my hand. I didn't step on the guy or hit the guy or anything else. The incident was over in a flash. That was it. Then the next day they went down and swore out a warrant for my arrest on assaulting this guy."

"The tension was terrible," Dees remembered. "I walked out and down the stairs. They were pushing and shoving me. I held my hands up to protect myself. One of them dropped his hat to the floor and said I hit him. Two or three deputies were standing around, but they wouldn't do a darn thing."

Dees and his group were trapped in the courthouse. They feared that if they went to the empty, largely unobserved basement parking lot, the Klansmen could easily attack them. Dees wanted to ask the then-governor, Jim Hunt, to send in the highway patrol to ensure his group's safe conduct. He called a friend in Washington for help, and the friend immediately began calling Raleigh television stations and newspaper reporters.

Once back in the Raleigh courtroom, Dees loudly announced that before taking the next deposition, his group needed to go to the courthouse law library. Dees and his colleagues left the room — but once out of sight of the Klan, they ducked down the back stairs, ran to their car, and high-tailed it out to the airport.

But the harassment of Dees did not end there. In December 1984, guards on a routine patrol around the Dees house caught a man in full military garb, carrying a weapon, in their spotlight. "He was running across the property," Dees said. "They could have shot him" — but they didn't. On another occasion, a man was spotted in the trees across the road from Dees's home, and in yet another incident, a man in fatigues, his face blackened, was seen running across the lawn.

Later, an imprisoned Klansman who had decided to tell all at his bail hearing testified that he had been asked to get information on Dees in order to set the lawyer up for assassination. The Klansman, Billy Riccio, met with Dees in prison and, claiming he wanted to repent, told him he had attended a war council of far-right underground leaders at Glenn Miller's Angier, North Carolina farm the day after Dees took Miller's deposition. Riccio said Mike Norris, a member of the National Alliance who was in prison for harboring a fugitive, had been delegated to kill Dees. Riccio told Dees that Louis Beam was at the meeting.

The threats against Dees continued. Just before he made another court appearance in Raleigh, North Carolina, Klan watchers tapped into Miller's computer network, and, via that linkup, into the Aryan Nations' grid. Through the network, they discovered that the North Carolina Klan was attempting to find out where Dees would stay in Raleigh during the trial. Thoroughly alarmed, Dees asked a federal judge in Raleigh for help. The judge ordered Miller to stay clear of Dees, and ordered that all future depositions be taken in the federal grand jury room under armed guard.

Miller eventually agreed to an injunction against paramilitary activity in the state, and ultimately became a federal informant. In the end run, Dees won a civil suit against the Klan, resulting in a substantial financial settlement that brought the Klan to its knees.

Posse
Country

CHAPTER 4

Posse Country

On a camping trip to northern Mexico not long ago, a group of American patriots reportedly climbed a ridge of hills and, looking over to the other side, were amazed to see thousands of Soviet tanks in training. As they made their way back to camp, they were startled to see MIGs zipping across the sky. Back home, the campers called the State Department to alert the U.S. government to what they took to be plans for an imminent invasion. To their surprise and anger, the diplomats shrugged off the story, then asked them to keep the information to themselves.

The incident set these patriotic citizens to thinking: Wasn't it interesting that all roads in Mexico converged at Laredo, Texas, where there was a seven-lane-wide highway across the Rio Grande into the U.S.? Why had Mexico nationalized all railroads, and made the tracks converge at four points on the U.S. border? They remembered reading stories that told of tens of thousands of Russian horse troops sequestered just across the Bering Strait, and hearing of 80,000 Mongolian troops on the Baja Penninsula. And not long ago, a well-informed speaker passing through had brought news of 35,000 Vietcong troops in south Texas.

REGUARDING YOUR RESPONSE TO THE LAKE CO. SHERIFFS POSSE COMITATUS, THAT WAS YOUR SIGNATURE TO YOUR DEATH WARRANT.

YOU WILL HANG SHORTLY, IF YOU LIVE LONG ENOUGH.

YOUR TREASON WILL BE REWARDED JUST AS TREASON WAS 200 YR AGO.

AMERICANS
CONCERNED
FOR
FREEDOM AND
LIBERTY

DALLAS CHAPTEP
U.S.A.

The Posse Comitatus issued this death threat in 1976 to a
U.S. Senator, whose name was blacked out by the FBI.

These were the kinds of wild and ominous rumors spread by the Posse Comitatus across the Midwest in the 1980s. These improbable tales reinforced the conspiricist thinking that gripped the heartland, offering, for the moment, what seemed to be the hidden truth behind the chaotic times that had befallen so many farmers and small-town residents. The idea was that what was happening to them was part of a wider skein of events that was leading up to nuclear war, armed invasion, and — for those who were Christian believers — the final war of Armageddon and the return of Christ. Any number of groups and individuals were bringing news of the imminent great invasion, but all were connected to an underground movement called the Posse Comitatus.

Who Are Those Guys?

The Posse Comitatus was first organized in Portland, Oregon in 1969 by Henry L. Beach, who had just retired from the dry cleaning business. During the 1930s Beach was the state liaison officer for William Dudley Pelley's Silver Shirts, the storm trooper group formed immediately after Hitler took power in Germany.

The Posse believes all politics are local. Beach argued that the county sheriff is the highest legitimately elected official in the land, and that the sheriff has the right to form a posse including any able-bodied man over the age of eighteen. To the Posse the sheriff is, in reality, the executive branch of government. He directs law enforcement, including the empanelling of juries.

Like other constitutional fundamentalists, the Posse Comitatus thinks the federal government has far exceeded the limits prescribed in the Constitution, and that by means of a coalition of lawyers and judges, the government has violated the basic terms on which the country was founded. The federal government, for example, has no constitutional right to intercede in education; nor does it have the right to coin money that is not based on gold or silver. Nonetheless, the federal government has unlawfully delegated the power to coin money and fix the standard of weights and measures to the Federal Reserve System, which, as a Posse Comitatus Kansas bulletin put it, is "a private monopoly which neither the people nor the states authorized in the constitution." The Federal Reserve, in turn, is controlled by a cabal of international Zionist bankers who have profited from the

OFFICIAL POSSE BADGE

NOW AVAILABLE
For members only

Orders must be placed by authorized
agent of the Posse

Information packet $1.00

The Kansas Christian Posse.
By LAW of U.S. CONSTITUTION.

For Information Write,

Kansas Christian Posse
Box 205,
Holton, Ks. 66436

Posse Comitatus Handbook

THE POSSE COMITATUS
by authority of
The Constitution Of The United States

In the formation of this constitutional republic, the county has always been and remains to this day, the TRUE seat of the government for the citizens who are the inhabitants thereof. The County Sheriff is the only legal law enforcement officer in these United States of America.

The Sheriff can mobolize all men between the ages of 18 and 45 who are in good health and not in the federal military service. OTHERS CAN VOLUNTEER! This body of citizens is the Sheriff's Posse. Each must serve when called by the Sheriff. The title of this body is the Posse Comitatus.

The Posse is the entire body of those inhabitants who may be summoned by the Sheriff, or who may volunteer, to preserve the public peace or execute any lawful precept that is opposed. Since the Sheriff is the servant of the citizens who are inhabitants of the County, it is not his choice as to whether or not the Posse is organized and brought into being. It is only his choice as to whether or not he wishes to use it.

Since the formation of our Republic, the local County has always been the seat of government for the people. A county government is the highest authority of government in our Republic as it is closest to the people, who are in fact, the government. The County Sheriff is the only legal law enforcement officer in the United States. . . . It is his responsibility to protect the people of his County from unlawful acts on the part of anyone, including officials of government. His oath of office is to uphold, preserve and defend the constitution of these United States and the State in which his County Exists. He may be required to do no less and no more in the performance of his official duties. It should be emphasized that this protection extends to Citizens who are being subjected to unlawful acts even by officials of government, whether these be judges of courts or Federal or State Agents of any kind whatsoever.

The County Sheriff must be advised of the instances where unlawful acts are committed. It is the duty of the Sheriff to protect the local citizens from such unlawful acts. Once he has been advised and refuses to perform his lawful duty in respect to the matter, the Posse Comitatus has the lawful right under natural law to act in the name of the Sheriff to protect local jurisdiction. Since the Second Amendment to the Constitution says, "the right of the people to keep and bear arms shall not be infringed." In the execution of the law, arrests may be made. The criminal may be remanded to the custody of the County Sheriff for trial by a citizen jury empanelled by the Sheriff from citizens of the local jurisdiction . . .

The unlawful use of County Sheriffs as LACKEYS of the Courts should be discontinued at once. *There is no lawfull authority, for Judges and the Courts to direct the law enforcement activities of a County Sheriff. The Sheriff is accountable and responsible only to the citizens who are the inhabitants of his County.* He is under oath of office and need not receive unlawful orders from Judges or the Courts. They are the Judiciary but *the Sheriff is the Executive branch of our government.* He is responsible to protect citizens, even from unlawful acts of officials of government. If he refuses to do so, he should be removed from office promptly. . . .

The Constitution is a simple document. It says what it means and means what it says. It means today what it meant when it was written. It is the SUPREME LAW for the States of the Union as well as for the Federal Government, which has been created by the States and the people, existing as *States, which are separate sovereign Republics within the United States* . . . The Federal government is a servant of the States and the people, not their master. . . .

expansion of both communism (by manipulating the Soviet Union) and democracy (by manipulating the United States).

The income tax, too, is a violation of the Constitution and only the states, not the federal government, have the right to declare martial law. Such "violations," according to Posse thinking, are made possible by a corrupted court system, overseen by the Supreme Court, which in reality should answer to the dictates of the people's courts. "The highest court in the land is the Justice of Peace Court, which is closest to the people," according to a Posse Comitatus bulletin.

Posse rhetoric is also infused with Christian Identity theology which, as noted earlier, teaches that whites are the true descendants of the lost tribes of Israel and that Jews, blacks, and other minorities have sprung from Satan and are subhuman. Jewish bankers and their illegal organizations, such as B'nai B'rith, are thought to be at the heart of the conspiracy against the midwestern farmers. Tirades against Jews have been standard Posse doctrine: "Yahweh our father is at work setting the stage for the final act against the Christ-murdering Jews and their father, Satan," begins a screed by Jim Wickstrom, the Wisconsin Posse leader and Christian Identity preacher who by 1985 was the most visible national Posse figure. The sermon also warns that "The Jews who control the Federal Reserve control the availability of food."

A typical radio broadcast on a Posse-controlled Kansas radio station began: "[The Bible] didn't say you're gonna vote them out — it said, 'thus with violence shall that great city Babylon — that international communist system — be thrown down and shall be found no more. . . .' And all the disco bongo congo from the bongo is gonna be gone. All the nigger jive and the tootsie wootsie is going to go."

During the early 1970s, Beach was the Posse's chief proponent, and he spent most of his time printing and mailing thousands of pages of Posse literature to members across the country. "The Posse concept is now becoming a nation-wide movement," Beach said in a set of Posse instructions. "To date we have posses in nearly every state. In some cases we are supplying the books to sheriff's departments and in one case to a judge which is actively interested. We recommend sending one of the Posse books to every sheriff in your state, also the governor, legislators, and every commissioner. It is effective, and is causing them to take a second look at their activities, which they know

The "WOODLAWN ORGANIZATION", a coalition affiliate in Chicago stated; "SO WE'RE LIKELY TO SEE ORGANIZED GUERILLA WARFARE, STRIKING OUT TO DOWNTOWNS AND OTHER AFFLUENT CITY AREAS."

This guerilla warfare no doubt will be led by the Jew communist specially trained Soviet and Cuban agents along with the thousands of Viet Cong that the Jews, who control the Immigration Department has allowed into the United States.

THE POSSE

It's time for old-fashioned
American Justice

The scene at the left will be a very common situation in rural America when and if the above information takes place. The White Anglo/Saxon Posse's across this Christian Republic await for the opportunity to clean up America of which the Jews and their 'lackey' jerks called politicians have made a GARBAGE DUMP.

- - - - - - - - - -

On or near May 10, 1983 there will be a LARGE INTERNATIONAL BANKING MEETING to reshape the 'world' banking system. This should be very interesting. I'm suprised that it wasn't scheduled for May 1st (MAY DAY-COMMUNISISM) of which is of the Jewish bankers.

Store guns, ammunition, and other supplies while they are yet available...... it is far later than you think. Praise YAHVEH, our King of Kings. Remember.... Luke 19:27, and the weekly information number to call.... (715) 535-2828.

REPRINT PERMISSION GRANTED
PASS ON TO A FRIEND

James P. Wickstrom
National Director of Counter-Insurgency

---

are actions of treason." A Posse charter required signatures of "seven male Christians" who would be "the guiding hand" in forming the Posse and "hopefully keep the Posse under control."

Beach claimed a Posse membership of 100,000 and, while no one ever took that claim seriously, Posse members built a reputation for themselves.

In 1974 Thomas Stockheimer, chairman of the Wisconsin Posse, was convicted of assaulting an IRS officer. He fled and was apprehended three years later in West Virginia. In 1976, Posse members seized a potato-packing shed during a land dispute in Stansfield, Oregon. All during the 1970s, Wisconsin Posse members disrupted meetings of the Department of Natural Resources in that state. It was viewed as a particular enemy because of its supposed manipulation and poisoning of the water supply. In one incident a Wisconsin statehouse security officer was maced.

After the Little Rock, Arkansas FBI office reported a Posse threat against the life of Vice President Nelson Rockefeller in 1975, the Bureau opened an investigation. A 1976 FBI report estimated Posse membership at anywhere from 12,000 to 50,000 members with perhaps ten to twelve times that many sympathizers. There were seventy-eight chapters in twenty-three states, with considerable support in the Great Plains, where there

Posse leader and Christian Identity minister James Wickstrom recruiting for the Posse in Tigerton, Wisconsin in 1981.

Public Notice

THE TIME HAS COME

WITH OUR DEMOCRACY DETERIORATED INTO HYPOCRACY . . .

WITH VIOLENT CRIMES, MURDER, DOPE, RAPE, KIDNAPPING, HOLDUPS, ROBBERIES, CATTLE RUSTLING, VANDALISM, BEATINGS AND TORTURING OF PEOPLE, YOUNG AND OLD, AND ALL OTHER ACTS OF CRIME AND VIOLENCE . . .

WITH LITTLE OR NO RESPECT FOR LAW AND ORDER . . .

WITH LITTLE OR NO LAW ENFORCEMENT . . .

WITH LITTLE OR NO JUSTICE IN OUR JUDICIARY COURTS . . .

THE TIME HAS COME FOR ACTION

BY THE LAW-ABIDING CITIZENS OF MONTANA, AND ALL OF THE OTHER FORTY-NINE STATES OF OUR GREAT REPUBLIC OF THE UNITED STATES OF AMERICA.

IF THERE ARE ONE, TWO, THREE THOUSANDS OR MORE OF RED-BLOODED AMERICANS IN MONTANA WHO ARE WILLING AND INTERESTED IN BRINGING LAW AND ORDER, JUSTICE AND HONESTY BACK TO OUR STATE, WHO ARE WILLING TO FIGHT OR DIE FOR THEIR HOMES, SAFETY AND LOVED ONES, WILL THEY PLEASE CONTACT ME AT ONCE.

THERE WILL BE POSSE COMATATUS COMMITTEES, ORGANIZED THROUGHOUT MONTANA AND FORTY-NINE OTHER STATES OF OUR GREAT REPUBLIC OF THE UNITED STATES OF AMERICA VERY SOON.

ALL PERSONS INTERESTED IN ORGANIZING POSSE COMATATUS COMMITTEES AND ALL PERSONS BELONGING TO THIS ORGANIZATION MUST BE TWENTY-FIVE YEAR OF AGE OR OLDER, MARRIED AND OWN PROPERTY.

THEY MUST BE LAW-ABIDING CITIZENS WITH A CLEAN RECORD.

THERE WILL BE NO SHOOTINGS OR HANGINGS EXCEPT FOR MURDER, KIDNAPPING, RAPE AND CATTLE RUSTLING.

LESSER CRIMES WILL BE HANDLED ACCORDING TO THE SERIOUSNESS OF CRIMES COMMITTED.

PLEASE REMEMBER THAT IT WAS THE VIGILANTES, ORGANIZED OVER ONE HUNDRED YEARS AGO WHEN MONTANA WAS ONLY A TERRITORY, ORGANIZED BY OUR FOREFATHERS, THAT BROUGHT LAW AND ORDER TO MONTANA.

WHAT OUR FOREFATHERS DID OVER ONE HUNDRED YEARS AGO WE CAN AND MUST DO TODAY TO RESTORE LAW, ORDER, AND FREEDOM TO THE PEOPLE OF THE UNITED STATES OF AMERICA.

ALL CITIZENS INTERESTED IN POSSE COMATATUS COMMITTEES PLEASE CONTACT ME AS SOON AS POSSIBLE IN PERSON OR BY MAIL AT STEVENSVILLE, MONTANA, 59870.

SIGNED AND DATED THIS 24TH DAY OF APRIL, 1974 BY

Loren Nedley

CAPTAIN LOREN J.B. NEDLEY

were seriously depressed farm economies. There were Posse chapters in Kansas, Nebraska, North Dakota, Colorado, Idaho, Washington, Texas, California, Montana, Illinois, Delaware, and Michigan. Wisconsin, and in particular the town of Tigerton Dells, became the center of Posse activity. The organization had established ties with other far-right groups. "We work with Posses wherever we can," David Duke, then the head of the Knights of the Ku Klux Klan, told *Newsweek* in 1975. "We get their material and funnel it to our groups."

But it was in the 1980s that the Posse really came into its own. In June 1980, a Michigan Posse member was convicted of attempting to pass counterfeit money, and a witness at the trial said that the money was printed on a Posse printing press. The witness claimed the Posse had at least $500,000 in counterfeit bills. Later in 1980, James Wickstrom, the fiery, anti-Semitic Wisconsin Posse leader, ran for the Wisconsin state senate and got 16,000 votes. The next year, 300 Posse members were reported to be at a military training camp, and in 1982, forty people led by the Posse prevented a

The Only Flag

To Which We Pay Allegiance

IN GOD

Holy Bible

WE TRUST

I,_____, do solemnly swear to promote the purposes and principles of the SHERIFF'S POSSE COMITATUS, "to defend and uphold the Supreme Law of the Land, the Constitution of the United States of America and of the Sovereign State of Wisconsin, against ALL ENEMIES, foreign and domestic, and to support our duly-elected County Sheriffs in the performance of their lawful duties." As a duly-sworn member of the County Chapter of the SHERIFF'S POSSE COMITATUS, I do hereby pledge my sacred honor and alliegance to defend and uphold these principles.

SHERIFF'S POSSE COMITATUS

Date _____

_____
Member's Signature

_____
Officer--Witness

U.S. CONSTITUTION

Posse

BY LAW OF

Posse Comitatus

United States Citizens for Constitutional Rights

REDEEM THE REPUBLIC!

May 1981

In GOD We Trust

Posse Comitatus
Post Office Box 31
Evansville, WI 53536

Posse Noose Report

Throughout the United States, State Police units are storing a tremendous amount of food stuffs and medicines. The main police post for each state also has a complete computer network installed with names of Christian Patriots therein, waiting for orders to unleash their forces against fellow Americans. This will be a direct act of TREASON against "We the People", and these forces must be totally incapacitated at that time. . . . Since the State Police are storing food (compliments of the American taxpayer), then SOMEONE has forewarned them of the trouble coming. Why hasn't Christian America been forewarned??

Disposable BODY BAGS are now being distributed throughout the states . . . There is no food being stored in Civil Defense shelters, but they have a BODY BAG for everyone. . . .

Other short notes: An old fort near Nevada, Missouri that was used to house German prisoners of war is being totally refurbished, including new fence and guard towers. This is one of many throughout the United States. Who does the Federal Government (KGB) plan to put in these human warehouses?? To coincide with this information, many county mental institutions are PREPARING their staffs with new medicines for a "new type of inmate who are not violent but do not like the present Administration in Washington . . ."

It is strongly suggested that ALL Christian Americans purchase at least nine months of food for EVERYONE in the family, munitions, guns, and other supplies . . . It is better to be prepared early than a day too late!! . . . The Posse is growing in ranks . . . The middleclass workers are striding with us, having found out why they are unemployed. The corrupt Jewish money and banking system that has bankrupted this Christian republic is the cause for the illegal foreclosures of their property. . . .

The "Cashless Society" (bank computers) is now interlocked from East to West Coast. Each business can be connected with their electric cash register through a telephone hookup to their local bank computer. . . . Isn't it nice how Rockefeller and his Jewish cohorts have made it so easy. Only one thing wrong—many people are waking up to the scheme and also to the constitutionality of LAWFUL MONEY versus PHONEY MONEY and the LAWS and RIGHTS of "We the People". "Hangin Tree, oh Hangin Tree. . . ."

I have been warning the residents of Wisconsin that a money problem was imminent . . . The Federal Reserve System is a private banking system . . . that manipulates the international gold and silver

standard in the world. . . . [It] is run and controlled by the Rockefellers and can create the recessions and depressions at will. . . .

Resolution #6, dated December 9, 1975, from Wood County, Wisconsin enabled the Conservation and Forestry Emergency Government to "establish an interim burial site on county owned land for use in mass county disasters." . . . "The Wood County Emergency Operations plan, as officially adopted by the County, requires provisions for an emergency mortuary service (bulldozers), which includes establishment of a temporary burial site for *mass casualty dead* . . . Recent reports have told of hundreds of thousands of people from urban locations that would be shipped north in an emergency.

Add it up:

1. Planned crisis by: monetary crisis through the banks, internal Jewish communist revolution, or limited Soviet nuclear attack upon major military installations and industrial cities.
2. Mass evacuation into preselected rural host areas. In the Civil Defense Preparedness Manual, Point #1 stresses no firearms permitted by evacuees.
3. Civil Defense Shelters have been emptied of food, medicines and other survival equipment.
4. Rural host areas have established mass burial sites. Massive amounts of disposable body bags have been distributed.

Please bear in mind that the Jews controlling our government on the local, state, and federal level, are selling the American people down the river.

Matt. 12:34-37
John 8:41-47
Luke 19:27

ARM EVERY AMERICAN
THERE ARE CRIMINALS ON THE LOOSE IN WASHINGTON

No man escapes when freedom fails.
The best men rot in filthy jails.
And those who cried, "Apease, apease,"
Are hanged by those they tried to please.

James P. Wickstrom
James P. Wickstrom
National Director of Counter-Insurgency

PASS ON TO A FRIEND   REPRINTED PERMISSION GRANTED

Wallace County, Kansas sheriff from repossessing farm equipment. Three Posse members were convicted in Colorado of manufacturing explosives. In February of 1983 a man identifying himself as a Posse member threatened to bomb a Johnson, Kansas school unless the sheriff and under-sheriff turned themselves in for execution. In November the 105 county sheriffs in Kansas received letters demanding that they arrest ten judges who had been guilty of various crimes including unlawfully seizing personal property. The "indictment" was signed by the Citizens Grand Jury of Kansas, and said, "If the county jails are denide [sic] by the county sheriffs for incarcerations of said outlaws, or the act of deceit is used to free said outlaws by the sheriffs then said outlaws will be buried in Potters field." Beginning in 1982 the Dodge City, Kansas radio station KTTL ran two regularly scheduled thirty to forty–minute programs featuring Posse speakers, including Wickstrom and William Gale, the California Christian Identity minister. The station was owned by Charles and Nellie Babs, both reputedly members of the Posse.

CITIZENS LAW ENFORCEMENT & RESEARCH COMMITTEE

H. L. (Mike) Beach
Phone: (503) 281-2043

C. L. E. R. C.
3530 N. E. Lombard Ct.
Portland, OR. 97211

In early 1983, Springfield, Colorado was the scene of a near-riot led by Posse members trying to block an auction of a local member's farm. Then, on a fog-shrouded night in February 1983 in North Dakota, two federal marshals were killed in a shootout with several Posse members. Their leader, Gordon Kahl, slipped away into the countryside.

Kahl and Humphreys

A decorated hero in World War II, Gordon Kahl first heard about the so-called international Jewish conspiracy in North Carolina, where he was serving out his tour of duty as a gunnery instructor. As James Corcoran tells the story in *Bitter Harvest*, Kahl then read Henry Ford's *The International Jew*. After the war Kahl worked the family homestead in North Dakota during the spring and summers, and travelled to California or Texas during the winters to work as a car mechanic or in the oil fields. In 1964 in North Dakota he learned about the tax protest movement; finally, in 1974 in Texas he was introduced to the Posse. He joined, announced his intention not to pay taxes, and in 1976 went on television to urge others to join him. He was quickly arrested, charged, and convicted of tax evasion, and sent to the federal prison at Leavenworth for a year, then released on probation. In the early 1980s he returned to North Dakota, where the IRS had seized some of his land. One of the terms of his probation was that Kahl would stay away from the Posse. But he paid no attention to the stipulation, and continued to travel around the Midwest warning people of the Jewish conspiracy. Eventually the government issued a warrant for his arrest for violating the terms of probation.

It was on February 13, 1983, on a narrow

The Medina Shootout

[Posse leader Gordon Kahl recounts the deadly 1983 shootout in Medina, North Dakota, between the Posse and Federal marshals. Two months later, Kahl himself was killed by SWAT teams in Arkansas.]

I, GORDON KAHL, a Christian patriot, and in consideration of the events which have taken place within the last few hours, and knowing to what length the enemies of Christ, (who I consider my enemies) will go to seperate my spirit from it's body, wish to put down on paper a record of the events which have just taken place, so that the world will know what happened. . . .

We had just finished our meeting in Medina, concerning how we could best impliment the proceedings of the Third Continental Congress, which was to restore the power and prestige of the U.S. Constitution up to and including the 10 Articles of the Bill of Rights, and put our nation back under Christian Common Law, which is another way of saying God's Law, as laid down by the inspiration of God, thru His prophets and preserved for us in the Scriptures, when word was received from someone whose identity I am not able to give, that we were to be ambushed on our return to our homes. . . .

As we came over one of the hills just north of Medina, I saw on the top of the next hill what looked like two cars parked on it. About this time they turned on their red lights, and I knew the attack was under way.

We were just coming to an approach and I told Dave to pull in on it and stop. Our other car pulled in just beyond us and stopped, also. I looked back in time to see another vehicle coming from behind with it's red light on. I picked up my Mini-14, and got out and got myself and my weapon ready as the vehicle coming from behind skidded to a stop about 20 feet away. The doors flew open on it and the two men who were in the front seat aimed their guns at us. My son Yorie had jumped out of the other car and had ran over to a high-line pole. The two cars which we had seen ahead us, pulled up and stopped behind us.

A man got out of the vehicle which had come from behind us, and ran out into the ditch on the east side of the road. During this time there was a lot of screaming and hollering going on but nothing else so it appeared to be an impasse.

About this time a shot rang out, and the driver of the car who I believe at this time must have been supposedly in command, turned around and stood up so he was looking at his man in the east ditch, and toward the cars which had come from the north and yelled, "Who fired, who fired?" The other man who was with him, echoed his question.

At the time the shot rang out I heard Yorie cry out "I'm hit, I'm hit". I took my eyes off the two men who were yelling "Who fired?", and looked over at Yorie. He was still standing, but I could tell he was in pain from the way he stood. About this time, another shot rang out, and I heard Yorie cry out again. I looked over and saw that he was hit again and laying on the ground. I looked back toward the two men and saw the one in the passenger side aim at me and I was sure then that they felt the situation was no longer under their control, and the only thing to do was kill us all. Before he was able to fire, I loosed a round at the door behind which he was standing, and while I don't think I hit him, it caused him to duck down behind the door.

I looked around again toward Yorie, and saw Scotty Faul running over toward him. I turned my head again in time to see the driver of the vehicle which had followed us raise up from behind his door and aim his gun at Scotty. I moved my gun over and fired at him before he could shoot. I didn't hit him either, the bullet striking somewhere near the lower left hand corner of the windshield. He ducked down behind the dash so I could only see his head. About this time the other man raised up and aimed at me again. I shot again striking the door and causing him to duck. This happened several times, . . . until the man on the passenger side fell, and I was able to tell he was out of the fight. The driver must have seen this as he moved his gun from Scotty's direction toward me.

I fired several more shots, at him each time he raised up to shoot at me. I finally realized this could keep up 'til my 30 round clip was empty. My bullets appeared to be ricocheting off the windshield and door post. I ran around toward the side of the vehicle, firing at the door as I went to keep him down until I got around far enough to get a clear shot at him, at which time I know he was out of the fight also.

I ran back where I could see the third man from this north-bound vehicle just in time to see him raise up to shoot at Scotty, who had ran over to Yorie. Before he was able to pull the trigger I fired and he fell to the ground. At this I saw the man who was behind the front end of the green Mercury, raise up and aim at Scotty. He saw me swing my gun in his direction, and he ducked down behind his car. I could see his feet or legs beneath the car, and I fired, striking him and putting him out of the fight.

I ran over to the man in the east ditch, thinking he might still be in fighting condition. When I got nearly to him, he raised up his head and said "Don't shoot me again, I'm all done". He had his hand on his shotgun so I took that and his pistol which was in his holster and threw them in the back seat of the green Mercury. I didn't see the man who had been behind the Mercury, and who I thought I'd hit in the leg, so I don't know where he'd gone.

A pickup had pulled up behind the north-bound vehicle, but I didn't notice anyone in it or around it and I assume it was the pickup we saw on the top of the first hill as we came out of Medina, and which I believe belonged to the city, but as to who was driving it, I have no knowledge.

Scotty tells me he saw one and possibly two men run out into the trees and hide, but I have no way of knowing who they were. . . .

Yorie's .45 auto which he had in his shoulder holster had either a rifle or pistol bullet imbedded in the clip, shattering the grips on both sides. Had he not been wearing it he would have been killed instantly.

Whether this was the first or second shot that was fired at him I don't know. One was buckshot and the other was either a rifle or a high-powered pistol from the way the bullet looks.

I didn't see it, but it sounded as though Yorie's gun fired after he was hit. I think probably his finger tightened on the trigger when he was hit, but I know neither he nor Scotty fired before this, and whether either of them fired afterwards, I don't know. I know that if they did, they didn't hit anyone, as I *knew* when I hit each one of them, myself.

I saw a man in the clinic when we took Yorie in; who I think must have been the man in the pickup, who pulled up behind what I think was the marshals vehicle. He had blood on his face, and I think he was probably hit by either a bullet or bullets which glanced off the marshals' vehicle when I was firing at them. I didn't see him, and I know I didn't shoot at him, and I know neither Yorie nor Scotty shot at him.

Vernon Wagner was unarmed so I know he didn't shoot at anyone and Dave Brower didn't shoot at anyone either. My wife had nothing to do with it, other than the fact that she had rode along with us, so she could visit with a couple of other ladies who were coming to the meeting.

I want the world to know that I take no pleasure in the death or injury of any of these people, any more than I felt, when I was forced to bring to an end, the fighter pilots lives who forced the issue during WW II. When you come under attack by anyone, it becomes a matter of survival. I was forced to kill an American P-51 pilot one day over Burma, when he mistook us for Japs. I let him shoot first, but he missed and I didn't. I felt bad, but I knew I had no choice.

I would have like nothing other to be left alone, so I could enjoy life, liberty and the pursuit of happiness, which our Forefathers willed to us. This was not to be, after I discovered that our nation had fallen into the hands of an alien people, who are referred to as a nation within the other nations. As one of our Founding Fathers stated, "They are vampires, and vampires cannot live on vampires, they must live on Christians". He tried to get a provision written into the U.S. Constitution that would have prevented Jews living inside the U.S. He warned his brethren that if this was not done their children would curse them in their graves, and that within 200 years, their people (the Jews) would be setting in their counting houses rubbing their hands, while our people would be slaving in the fields to support them. This has happened exactly as was predicted.

These enemies of Christ have taken their Jewish Communist Manifesto, and incorporated it into the Statutory Laws of our country, and threw our Constitution and our Christian Common Law (which is nothing other than the Laws of God as set forth in the Scriptures), into the garbage can.

We are a conquered and occupied nation; conquered and occupied by the Jews, and their hundreds or maybe thousands of front organizations doing their un-Godly work. They have two objectives in their goal of ruling the world. Destroy Christianity and the White race. Neither can be accomplished by itself, they stand or fall together.

We are engaged in a struggle to the death between the people of the Kingdom of God, and the Kingdom of Satan. It started long ago, and is now best described as a struggle between Jacob & Esau.

I would like to write more but the Spirit says this must suffice for now. Should the hand of Elijah's God continue over me, and protect me, I shall someday see this once great nation swept clean of Christ's enemies, and restored to it's former greatness. If it should be the will of *our* Father, and the Father of our Lord Jesus Christ, that this be, there will be no way that Ahab's god and his people can stand before us. Mystery Babylon with all it's greatness, will be destroyed. Take heart, my fellow Christian Americans, God has said that there will be a great shaking in the Land of Israel. That started this evening. Let each of you who says that the Lord Jesus Christ, is your personal Saviour, sell his garment and buy a sword, if you don't already have one, and bring His enemies before Him and slay them.

If you've been paying tithes to the Synogogue of Satan, under the 2nd plank of the Communist Manifesto to finance your own destruction, stop right now, and tell Satan's tithing collectors, as I did many years ago, "Never again will I give aid and comfort to the enemies of Christ". To those of you who were engaged in the ambush and attack on us and were spared, thank God you have a chance to remove your support from the Anti-Christs who rule our nation.

To those of you who are or have been supporting the Edicts and Commands of the Great Whore—Stop now and come out of her, as her time is getting short and when the hour of her judgment comes, that you be not judged with her.

I must cease now, and move on. If it should be the will of the Father that I have more to do for Him, He will protect me, and no devise whatever that is used against me shall succeed. To my wife Joan, who has been with me for so long, I know this will be a hard and painful experience; however, remember that prophecy will be fulfilled, and that you have now been a witness to some of it. Remember that I love you as much today as I did when I first saw you more than 50 years ago. Put your trust in God, and whether I live or die, He will be with you to the end of your days.

To my son Yorie and my dear friend Scotty—you both displayed the qualities of first rate soldiers of Jesus Christ. May God bless all of you.

I must now depart—I have no idea where I'm going, but after some more prayer, I will go where the Lord leads me, and either live to carry on the fight, or die if that be the case, and for the present at least, I bid you all good-bye.

Gordon Kahl, Christian Patriot

country road leading out of Medina, North Dakota, that two federal marshals were killed and three others wounded in a shootout with several Posse members who had just left a meeting to organize a Posse township (from which, Kahl had argued, all minorities should be excluded). After the shooting, Kahl slipped away into the countryside. Months later he was tracked down by federal lawmen in Arkansas and killed in a gunfight.

The following year Arthur Kirk, a Nebraska farmer, was facing foreclosure. He was known as a Posse sympathizer, and had threatened to shoot it out if the sheriff actually sought to repossess his farm. A Nebraska State patrol SWAT team was sent to Kirk's farm, and he was shot and killed.

Both Kirk and Kahl soon became Posse martyrs. In Kansas and Nebraska, conservative estimates put Posse sympathizers in one-third of all the sheriff's departments. Local and state police in Nebraska began to share intelligence on Posse activities with the FBI, and in 1985, when a group of armed men suddenly appeared in rural Georgia, throwing up a perimeter defense around the farm of a poor — and, surprisingly, black — farmer who was about to lose his land in foreclosure, the Posse leaped into the national news.

The leader of the group was Larry Humphreys, a young, handsome, former professional pool hustler from Oklahoma. For a brief moment in history he became a plains hero, travelling from one rightwing farm meeting to another, promising to rescue farmers confronting foreclosure.

Humphreys grew up in Duncan, Oklahoma, the son of a local banker who had made a fortune in oil. When Humphreys got into trouble with drugs as a teenager, his family shipped him off to a boarding school in New Jersey. He returned and briefly attended college in Oklahoma, then ran a bar in Vail, Colorado, and eventually ended up as a world-class pool player. He travelled around the country gambling, and finally settled down in Houston.

It was in Houston during the 1970s that Humphreys, as he put it, "got conviction" and underwent a period of religious transformation. It was then that he discovered "the conspiracy." Humphreys's understanding of the conspiracy began with a reading of the story of the Illuminati and the purported eighteenth-century European Freemasons plot for world domination. A cursory reading of the histories of the Federal Reserve System and the Trilateral Commission seemed to fit in perfectly. In short, Humphreys had hit upon the fabled Jewish international banking conspiracy. "It's pretty much common knowledge that most of the international banks are Jewish," he has said. "But regardless of whether or not it is a Jewish conspiracy per se, there are only a few people involved. The vast majority of their [Jewish] people don't know what is happening."

When an Associated Press reporter asked Humphreys, in 1985, whether he shared the white supremacist views of the neo-Nazis, he replied: "I believe the Anglo-Saxon and Celtic people trace their ancestry to the Bible and have a responsibility to administer divine law." He elaborated on that in another interview with the *Dallas Morning News*: "The idea that we [whites] are the Israel people does not put us in a superior position to other people so that we should look down on other races. . . . In fact, we have more responsibility . . . to show them the blessing. . . . The Bible's principles apply to all nations. But its covenants apply to us."

Where many fundamentalist Christians look forward to the last great battle of Armageddon and the second coming of Christ, Humphreys believed the world had been immersed in Armageddon for

AT LAST! WE HAVE A HERO!
Gordon Kahl — The First American Hero — Of The Second American Revolution

It's over. It's done. Gordon Kahl has died this night in a heroic struggle for freedom and liberty. One man has stood like a Travis or Crockett ti hurl his defiance at the government which has now become the enemy of the people. Ring the bells. Sound the war trumphet, a soldier of our Race has died. Visions of vikings standing at the gate to Valhalla — arms outstreched in salute to another brave warriour.

Listen! Leonidas calls! "Who is this man that dares to equal the courage of my brave three hundred? Who is this that so boldly treads upon the ground where my men have stood in blood stained honor for 2500 hundred years." No answer.

Salute! Twelve thousand heels slam togather. A shadowey figure steps forward and plants the standard — SPOP. "In the name of the Senate, with what legion do you serve ..." No answer.

A trumpet sounds. A mighty charger comes rushing forward. A loud riotous laugh echos as from amidst a hundred Saracens the red — dragoned Richard rides forth — his sword yet driping. "Three words have I for you: "God Wills It!"

Tramp, Tramp, Tramp. Ten thousand men march through pristine snow. Scarlet it turns, for their feet are bare. "All Halt!" A large noble — looking man, with kindly eyes looks upon the stranger. "Come, my son, join freedom's legion. We shall stand on Trenton's shore before the moring comes." No answer.

Silence. The mournful notes of Deguallo can be heard across the square. The flag of 1824 snaps in the wind. Wait! Who is this that steps between poised Mexican hoard and defiant Anglo band. "Come here to the parapet! stand with us and forever write your name on history's immortal page," shouts a determined Texan. No answer.

"Fix bayonets! Step forward on the comand!" Countless gray — clad men gaze toward Little Round Top. Silently they prepare iron will to meet iron and stele. General Pickett raises his sword. The sun glistens, shimmering from the blade. Time stands still for a moment, all of eternity hanging from the blade. "You, Sir, come stand with my men, for you can this day insure that your name will forever be spoken by admiring men." No answer.

Late winter's eve. Lonely road leading into the darkness. Foe lies in hiding ambush. Hell's children prepare to strike. Shamessly they plan to kill; for the government that once was the handmaiden of liberty has now become the mistress of slavery. Piercing eyes! Warriour's heart! Stand aside, freedom's foe! Despots dead and tyrants dying. "All of history's brave who called, Behold! my answer to your queries. See now my tracks upon the sands of time. Here is my time, my fate. I choose to stand because others have feared. My countrymen led deep into the tunnel of eternal slavery; I now lead them out with light from the barrel of my Mini—14. Soon I, too, shall be where you repose. But first I light sacred liberty's torch."

Born in blood this Nation was. Reborn in blood it now shall be.

An Ode to Gordon Kahl, by Louis R. Beam Jr.
(Gordon, save a place with the Master for
me, for even now others pledge their honor
to follow you to Glory.)

most of the twentieth century, and would soon enter an era of peace. His melange of religious and political interests got Humphreys "kicked out" of his local Baptist church, branded a "heretic" and a "cult leader."

If the Posse itself was never a large organization, it nonetheless achieved mythic stature, and became a political metaphor to such an extent that Posse symbolism pervaded mainstream politics across the Midwest. The Posse became a symbol of resistance to the spreading "tyranny" of the state, which was manifested by the banks taking over farms. The Posse member became a symbol of the patriot, of the sovereign who, in order to maintain his freedom, has become an outlaw in his own country.

Posse people talk tough, and they are usually armed to the teeth. The Posse is, oddly enough, a little like the New Left SDS was in the 1960s: It is a free-form movement, rather than a static party;

Larry Humphreys (center) after addressing a right-wing farm rally in Kearney, Nebraska in 1985.

Farmer Kirk's Last Words

[The following is an edited transcript of a telephone conversation between police officials and Posse Comitatus supporter Arthur Kirk, just before he was shot by a Nebraska police SWAT team in 1984.]

This is my home . . . How in the hell am I going to defend myself when I get out in the open?

I'm a damn German Irish, but I'm a mixed up mongrel but by God I've been learning how to shoot my whole life, defending myself my whole life. I've climbed the wall my whole life and damn you I'm not stopping now. You ain't going to walk over me until I'm cold and if you want to make me cold I'm not afraid of it. I've led a damn good life and I'm not ashamed of nothing I ever done. . . . Why all this God damn monkey business? Why don't you let me try and make a living?

Art, I don't have anything to do with what's . . .

God damn fuckin' Jews, they destroyed everything I ever worked for, I've worked my ass off for 49 God damn years and I've got nothing to show for it. By God, I ain't putting up with their bullshit now. I'm tired, and I've had it and I'm not the only God damn one, I'll tell you that. . . . Farmers fought the revolutionary war and we'll fight this son-of-a-bitch. We were hoping to do it in court but if you're going to make it impossible then damn you we'll take you on your own terms. . . . Keep your God damn tank, and your laser, your police airplane and harassing, buzz all over the place. I could have shot that son-of-a-bitch plane easy. Nothing to it. I caught me a goose at 75 yards just here the other day, it's not too God damn difficult to bring down a Cessna at 600 feet. Fly that son-of-a-bitch over here and fuck around with me, you'll find out about it. You just want to cock suck and screw around and I'll bring that son-of-a-bitch down like a God damn goose. You think I can't, just try me out.

Yeah, but nobody wants to do that Art. . . . basically what they want, they want you to go to court.

Who does?

Apparently something on the papers that they brought out to you deals with some sort of court hearing, Art.

Jesus Christ, I've been trying to get them in court. They squirm and bellyache around like a typical God damn luciferized bastard. I'm not afraid to meet em in court, but by God I'll have my PPK on my hip. You son-of-a-bitches are armed so will I be, and if you want to shoot me go ahead, but I'll carry that bastard into the court room. If you can carry em so can I. Got to protect myself someway.

Art, that's part of our job is to protect people.

That's right and you sure and the hell ain't doing a very good job for me. Norwest bank and the Jews are doing fine. You broke every damn right I got. . . .

Why did you come up on posted property without any authorization? Wouldn't even step back and explain to me what you done. That's all I ask. I was told to quit pointing the gun dammit, he pointed the gun at me first. I got a right to defend myself and by God you tell me different.

I'm not telling you that you don't have a right to defend yourself.

Then why in the hell is he telling me he's going to arrest me like a big shot. Mr. Lieutenant huffin', puffin' striped yellow belly.

Until you can tell me what kind of papers you're serving and what you're up to like a man and then leave me alone, quit harassing me.

Art, first of all I don't serve papers, the second thing, the papers were there to deal something with you going to court and that's all I know Art.

I've been trying to get the court for Jesus Christ, ask Jan Steeple how long ago he told me to hire a lawyer. It did me one hell of a lot of good. You know what that son-of-a-bitch did? He lied to me, every turn in the road. Filthy lying member of the bar, outlaw bastards. I filed a suit against the God damn bank that's been misusing me for years and years and years, unbeknowned to me until I started reading the laws myself because there was no other way to do it. Cause if you don't do it yourself it don't get done, and that ain't nothing new to me, I've known that all my life and I found out them dirty rotten son-of-a-bitches have done everything despicable that they can think of to me. Everything you can think, it's unimaginable, it's covered by the U.S. Constitution and U.S. titles passed by Congress, the highest law making body in the land, and they tell me that my suit is meritless. I'm going to tell you something: if the Constitution and the laws Congress passes are meritless, them son-of-a-bitches are completely discredited . . . They spent a week in Lincoln to formulate a stupid statement like that and then they come out here harassing me. I've got a pretty good idea that's what it's all about. Pointed guns at me and then saying something because I point one back, well shit. . . . You bring my wife up here and you put your God damn gun in the mailbox, let me search you, and we'll talk. I ain't taking none of your damn tricks, leave your fuckin' handcuffs stuck up somebody's butt. You ain't going to cuff me and fuck me around like some God damn hog in a pig sty. That's Lucifer's favorite trick. Nail again. I'm not one of your game, you know what I am. I'm an Israeli.

You're a what?

I'm a son of Abraham. Just what Lucifer claims he claims my birth right and that's a dirty rotten lie. He's born a king. I'll have none of his shit. Norwest bank is run by, where did they get all the power, who's got power of the world, how come the God damn Jews stink and go and farm other people's nuclear plants and we just sit and say now boys, now boys, musn't do that. Who runs this world, you tell me. Think about it a little bit. Open your eyes and smell the coffee.

Art, it's obviously . . .

You're just egging son, you know who the Mossad is?

What's a masade?

Most ruthless son-of-a-bitches the world has ever known.

What's the definition of masade?

They're more ruthless than [Stalin's] NKVD and the Gestapo put together ever thought of being. It's the people who are running the whole damn show, that's who it is.

Well I've never heard of people referred to as a masade.

Well I don't suppose you have. The business you're in you probably don't want to hear either. It's too bad, there's a lot of good men that are going down the tubes. You're probably one of em. That don't mean I'm going to lay down for you and let you stomp on me.

I'm capable of representing myself, hell of a lot better than any bar member ever did, I can name you all kinds of names, that stinky rotten bar association stinks. They've discredited themselves completely as far as I am concerned. The Constitution of the United States is meritless, that's the stupidest statement anybody could make. You can't get lower down than that. I know nobody wants to even admit that there is a Constitution. There's a big move on to try to subvert the Constitution, to change the whole thing. Communism, that isn't communism it's Judaism. We're there and they're coming and we all meeting them big happy deal where Rockafellow and all the big shots running the whole damn thing. Well, I can tell you, they ain't running me. We're going to have to make some better arrangements and I'm in the process of trying and if this harassment is supposed to deter me, I'm telling you it has the opposite effect, and it ain't going to change, nothing is going to change. You just bring my wife up here.

different groups do different things, and are constantly forming, changing, fighting, disappearing, and re-forming. Some factions are consumed with Armageddon theology. Others are preparing to fight the great war of Armageddon against the Soviet Union from base camps in "survival zones." Still others have devoted their energies to learning how to represent themselves in court and help farmers make a stand against foreclosure. Some have plunged into the white underground.

If you're Posse you drop out of the state bureaucracy. You don't have a driver's license, because by taking away power over the constitutional right to drive on the highways, the overbearing government is acting in an unlawful manner. You find out how to get rid of your birth certificate and marriage license. You don't have a bank account and you don't pay taxes (although some Posse patriots anonymously send what they consider to be a "rightful" amount of money to the Defense Department each year). You keep your money in silver, the common man's metal. You barter. You might steal. You've got a semi automatic Ruger Mini-14 rifle which you can make fully automatic in a few minutes. You've got several thousand rounds of ammunition at home, along with more food and ammo cached in hiding places strategically scattered about the country.

The Posse has its own grapevine, and a variety of newsletters, journals, and *samizdat* publications. *The Upright Ostrich* is a spiffy little magazine crammed with ads and advice for Patriots who don't pay taxes, fight foreclosure, and invest in precious metals and stones. Posse members also avidly read the Liberty Lobby's *Spotlight*. And top-secret Posse news comes word-of-mouth from people in the know — like reports of miniature Soviet and U.S. submarines secretly meeting for summits every month under the ice at the North Pole.

The ultimate goal of the Posse is to make the state wither away by rearing a new generation that can't be traced: children with no birth certificates, who don't go to school, who grow up as true sovereigns under God and the American Constitution.

Snap Crackle Populists

By 1985, Beach's original Posse was subsumed into a bewildering assortment of groups and individuals ranging from the Christian Posse and the Montana Vigilantes to the Iowa Society of Education and the National Agricultural Press Association, all of which offered the standard constitutional fundamentalist doctrine against the income tax and the Jew-controlled Federal Reserve. By the end of the decade, the Posse had become the vehicle for a revival of nativist politics.

It was onto this chaotic scene that Willis Carto of the Liberty Lobby appeared with yet another political vehicle to be fueled by the energies of the Posse and other far rightists: a new political party, aimed at capturing the renegade, anarchistic, and racialist sentiments sweeping across farm country. It was called the Populist Party.

The party made an appeal to constitutional fundamentalists with its program to abolish the Federal Reserve System (Populists sued in Iowa federal court to put an end to the Federal Reserve) and by calling for an end to the income tax. In fact, the party was an amalgam of splinter groups, including the Constitution Party, the American Party of Indiana, the American Independent Party in California, various Klans, and Christian Identity groups in Indiana and Florida.

The party's first chairman was Robert Weems,

THE UPRIGHT OSTRICH

Volume 4, Number 4   April 1985

COMPLIMENTARY
ISSUE
WE HOPE YOU SUBSCRIBE

SHERIFF'S SALE

FORD

FARMERS

EUSTACE MULLINS: "The World Order" page 8

a Mississippi Klan leader, who took the reins in 1984. Willis Carto was a member of the Populists' National Executive Committee from the beginning, and Bill Shearer and his California American Independent Party were initially major factors in the party.

Populists admired politicians like former Idaho Congressman George Hansen, who was convicted of income tax violations, Idaho Republican senator and hard money advocate Steve Symms and, of course, Senator Jesse Helms of North Carolina. On the other hand, the Populists found themselves in hot competition with Lyndon LaRouche in the farm belt, where LaRouchites were running as candidates in state and local elections, hoping to pick up leverage in right-wing coalition politics.

The real energy behind the Populist Party was the *Spotlight*, the weekly tabloid published out of the Washington, D.C. Liberty Lobby offices on Capitol Hill, around the corner from the Supreme Court. Its twenty-eight pages were filled with news from an eclectic right-wing perspective: how the racketeering statutes could be used to stop abortions, home satellites as a way around the media monopoly, and an attack on the film *The Last Temptation of Christ*. Stories sometimes displayed a dash of populism, such as an approving piece on South Dakota Democratic Congressman Byron Dorgan's attack on leveraged buyouts. There was news of a Swedish cure for Alzheimer's disease, a "super pill" to beat cholesterol, and helpful household hints, such as tear gas security devices designed to stop intruders.

On April 23, 1984, under the headline "Reagan Orders Concentration Camps," the *Spotlight* reported finding ten huge prison camps located at key defense commands across the nation, citing information from "two trustworthy confidential sources — patriotic career army officers stationed at Fort Benning and Fort Chaffee." In addition to rounding up aliens and "security suspects" coast-to-coast, Operation Rex 84 — as *Spotlight* said it was code named — would detain and deport illegal immigrants. "But these sources say Rex 84 has another, even more closely guarded and carefully orchestrated objective," the *Spotlight* asserted, "to apply so-called C&C [capture and custody] measures against political opponents, resisters or even outspoken critics whom the administration considers 'dangerous.' "

According to Leonard Zeskind of the Center for Democratic Renewal, who has studied the Populists since the party's inception, internal division wracked the party from the start: Olympic star Bob Richards, its presidential nominee in 1984, quit campaigning after getting into a dispute with Carto. Then Shearer and Carto themselves fell to quarrelling, mostly over money. Shearer accused Carto of using the Populist Party as a "fund-raising scheme through which he could divert money to his various corporations." Shearer had Carto voted off the executive committee, and installed his daughter Nancy as party administrator. At one point, like rival religious factions touting false popes, Shearer and Carto registered two Populist Parties with the Federal Election Commission. Within a few years of its high-water mark in 1982, the party had broken apart. But Carto was used to this sort of internecine squabbling, and he proceeded to reorganize the Populists in Pennsylvania, leaving the farm belt behind. There, in 1987, 150 people from twenty-six states met. Former Congressman Hansen joined Louisiana's David Duke as a guest speaker. Duke eventually became the party's 1988 presidential nominee.

Showdown on the Rulo Farm

No matter how hard politicians tried to capture the Posse energy in above-board politics, it all too often distintegrated into gothic terror. The story of the Rulo farm began in May 1984. Cheryl Gibson, twenty-eight, gathered up her five children and left Lester, her husband of ten years, and their Robinson, Kansas house to go live with friends at the home of Mike Ryan, a truck driver in Whiting, some thirty miles away. In the subsequent divorce proceedings, the couple agreed on joint custody; the children would live with Cheryl, but Lester would have regular visitation rights. But the agreement didn't work out, and Lester complained that he was unable to see his children. Finally a local Brown County, Kansas judge called a hearing to resolve the matter. Cheryl failed to appear. By the time the judge issued an order for the state to take custody of the children, both mother and youngsters had vanished.

Lester Gibson grew distraught, increasingly anxious over the whereabouts of his young children. He sought help from the local police, but the cops, terming Gibson's plight a private domestic dispute, refused to become involved. His in-laws accused him of abusing his wife and children, accusations Lester Gibson steadily denied. From the beginning, Gibson had thought there was some explanation for Cheryl's disappearance other than the usual adjustments after a divorce.

For most of their married life the Gibsons had lived a simple existence, raising their kids to attend mass at the local Catholic church, where Cheryl worked in the children's program. Lester had a good job at a nearby grain elevator. Then something had changed. Cheryl stopped going to church. She began to stockpile vitamin pills, and macaroni and cheese replaced the beef and pork on the family dinner table. Cheryl now spurned pork as the "unclean meat of Satan." She sat for hours on the telephone with her mother, Bible on her lap, as the two of them puzzled over the meaning of the Scriptures.

"I'd come home and there was no dinner," Lester Gibson told reporters from the *Kansas City Times.* "She'd be reading the Bible. I'd ask her, 'Why are you reading the Bible all the time?' and she'd say that she wanted to learn more."

Gibson knew that Cheryl and others in her family attended private Christian Identity–sponsored Bible study meetings. Soon after she left, he discovered tape recordings of Posse leader Jim Wickstrom's screeds among her belongings.

The Posse was no secret in northeastern Kansas. On several different occasions in 1981 and 1982, Wickstrom had spoken publicly in Hiawatha, close to the Gibson home. A few miles away in Seneca, the Posse and Identity preachers held several meetings in 1984.

Gibson himself had first heard about the Posse in 1983, through a local locksmith. "I'd go down there from time to time to have work done on my chain saw," he said. "He'd have a Wickstrom tape playing. It was Christian Identity stuff. He recruits all the time.

"First they tell you how not to pay taxes. Then it's protesting farm foreclosures. Religion just kinda creeps in, like you have to know 'who's who and who's Jew.' If you read the Bible and understood the truth, then you'd know what's going on. But I didn't become involved. Then a neighbor comes by and says Cheryl's brother Jimmy is at these Bible-study sessions — but he would never come by and talk to us. Finally, at Christmas in 1983, Jimmy shows up packing a Bible in one hand and a Mini-14 [semiautomatic rifle] in the other."

In his efforts to get help, Gibson called the

Jim Wickstrom from the Pulpit

[The following excerpts are from a taped sermon made by Christian Identity minister and Posse leader Jim Wickstrom on Memorial Day in 1982.]

Look at the preachers. I'm a minister. Big deal. So what? And did you notice everything he says is gospel? Did you ever notice that? And even the doctor, too. We can't forget the doctors. Because they're the new man gods of sorcery right? That's correct. . . . They can't leave you alone, you Identity people for thinking what you want to think. They always have to come over and try and force their views on you from their pagan worship, out of these Lutheran churches and these Catholic churches, and these damn Jew synagogues. You're not entitled to think what you want to think. They want to tell you what to think, and when to go, and how to go about it! . . .

You Identity people, no matter where you are listening to this tape, building up yourselves on your most holy faith, praying in the holy spirit. Keep yourselves in the love of Yahweh, looking for the mercy of our Joshua unto eternal life. . . . Have no pity on those in office who have taken and destroyed your rights and have been responsible for the aborting of our children and the death of our sons with chemicals and the death of our sons in war and the stealing of our rights. You do not have pity on these. But you have pity on your own people. For then will come the test of compassion on your brethren. Remember Yahweh stated that when this is over every knee shall bend and every tongue shall confess that Yahweh is Joshua. And it states also that all his sons and daughters that will dwell in the New Jerusalem shall call upon the name of Yahweh. Every one shall know who they are. It's going to be very interesting. Many of us have family problems where the fathers or the brothers or the sisters or the mothers are continually on your back, continually trying to get you to turn from the truth. But the day shall come shortly when they shall find out they have been totally betrayed by their ministers and priests. And then they shall be part of that congregation which is spoken of in the Bible which shall seek out these ministers and these preachers and they shall KILL THEM for lying to the congregation. And it shall be so bad that even their own parents of these ministers and priests shall run them through with the sword for lying unto the people. . . .

Yes, our people have a lot of tears. How many people do you think in the United States today or last Friday, or shall we say tomorrow when the mailman comes again — of course, you know the postal department has been run since 1972 by the American Can Co. which is owned by Rothschild and has a bunch of finking Jews getting all the bucks and they're guaranteed a certain percent of profit every year no matter how bad they run the business — how many of these people do you think will get a notice in the mail that they are being foreclosed upon, either their car, their truck, their business, their house, their ranch, their farm? I'll lay odds there's going to be a whole bunch. . . .

If you stick together as Christian friends, then you've got something going. OK? But if you're all alone out there and you've got no help it gets pretty lonely doesn't it? . . . Remember, Jesus said in the latter days to gather yourself together with those of like mind and enter into prayer and solemn feast. He's telling you through Solomon that you must group together to have your strength . . . He's talking about strength in numbers and this is why I've gone throughout this nation, and traveled through the United States of America, and I've told people to assemble their supplies, their munitions and their food, and to gather at least a minimum of five families together when the violence and the crime erupts in this land. Because there is power with numbers. When you can start throwing lead across those fields out of those 30 shot semiautomatic 308s and 223s, I'm telling you those beehives and those little hornets will really make her go. But it's different if you're all alone. But when you've got five or six of those babies buzzing, I'm telling you you've got some strength. . . .

Doesn't the husband and wife have to work today just to pay the bills, but forget about the kids. We'll bring a bunch of niggers in from Africa for you to adopt. We'll bring a bunch of Vietnamese in, with all those diseases, that you can adopt and you can have 'em run around your house and sit on your throne, in your restrooms. And then when your friends come over they can sit on it and get the disease too. And we'll send 'em to school with those other children of your neighbors and they can pick up the syphilis and all the worms and everything else. And we can't forget the lice. That's right. Flied lice. . . .

Where did we go wrong? We went wrong with our diet, didn't we? People started liking that lobster and shrimp, didn't they? And all that juicy pork. All that pig acid. Get down 'n them bones and give you gout. Give you trichini so they can bore through your blood vessels and give you strokes. . . . You can tell a person who eats a lot of pork: He stinks. He's a stinking sweater. When you walk around him you can't even stand it. Because the stench that's comin' out of them pores in the pork puss. Do you ever notice that when you get on a good diet you don't hardly need any deodorant whatsoever? I use it, but it's all natural vitamin E. But all these other people are going out and buying this Right Guard and Left Guard, and all this aluminum stuff to shoot under their armpits, right? To kill all those bugs or whatever they got in there. . . . And it totally clogs your sweat pores up and does not allow the toxins to get out of your body. . . . And if the toxins can't get out they make you sick. People have headaches all the time. Because no matter what they do they've clogged up their main sweat pores, which are under their arms. And then when they go take a shower they think they're going to get all the poisons out of them, and they take that bar of Dove, which should be spelled pig, and they take that sweaty, slimy piece of pussey pork and they wash their whole body with that piece of pig. Did you ever notice the film on your body when you use that piece of soap? That's pork, you know. You're a greased pig when you come out, just like the nigger carrying the football down the field. Yahweh said you're not to touch the pig, its carcass, or have anything to do with it. . . . Get off this Dove and slove and all these other models of soap. Then they've got the one that shows the Irishman who's working up a horrendous stench, Irish Spring made by the kike. All made with pork. Get off it! Wash your body with something clean. . . .

There's only been eight million children that's been aborted in the United States. . . . Now the doctors are god. If they can take the life of a young baby, who says they can't take your life if they want? Where's the age limit? There is no age limit. Now they've got hospices. Now they're trying to sign a bill in Washington where elderly people if they so wish can sign a piece of paper and go to a special place and be terminated. Isn't that beautiful! We don't want old people around because they might tell their grandchildren that they didn't give foreign aid to their enemies and that they didn't pay a communist graduated income tax — sixth plank of the Communist Manifesto. And that all of their tax money in their township financed their school. It didn't finance social problems in Milwaukee and Green Bay and everywhere else. The Bible says here that the grandmothers shall teach the grandchildren the truth. How can they when they're locked up in the cattle barns called nursing homes . . .

cult awareness network in Kansas City, which suggested he call Denny Whelan. Whelan was an Omaha private detective who had gained a reputation in the rescue — or kidnapping, depending on your point of view — of youngsters caught up in cults. Whelan met Gibson at a truck stop and the two of them talked for five hours. Gibson agreed to pay Whelan $1,500, and Whelan took the case.

Gibson told Whelan he had already traced Cheryl and the children north from Whiting across the Nebraska state line to a farm in Rulo, a hamlet alongside the Missouri River. This farm was originally owned by Otho Stice, whose son Rick had raised hogs there. The farm failed, and on repossession, the bank sold it to Cheryl's brother, James Haverkamp, and one of his in-laws. Gibson's attorney, Ted Collins, contacted the Richardson County, Nebraska prosecutor and Gene Ramer, the county sheriff, asking them to act on outstanding Kansas warrants. He was seeking return of the children to state custody and the arrest of Cheryl, who was wanted on a felony charge for violating a parental custody agreement. Collins was surprised when neither the prosecutor nor the sheriff would act on the warrants. They told Collins that the Gibson affair was a domestic dispute in which they did not want to interfere. While Collins was considering what to do next, Cheryl and the children disappeared from the farm.

Gibson was becoming increasingly frustrated with his dealings with local police, county sheriffs, and state law enforcement agencies. "I talked to county sheriffs," he said, "and when I found a sheriff who wasn't too cooperative, I knew he wasn't a good one to talk to. I developed a paranoia myself, and I was told by a KBI [Kansas Bureau of Investigation] agent not to trust anybody in law enforce-ment because they didn't know who was in [the Posse] and who wasn't."

At this point, private eye Denny Whelan went to work. He distributed flyers of Cheryl and the children across the Midwest, and began to interview local law enforcement authorities, friends, and relatives. He also searched Mike Ryan's Whiting house, where he found order forms for guns, delivery slips, and bills for over $7,000 worth of ammunition.

From the beginning, Whelan was sure Cheryl and the kids were still on the Rulo farm. And, he recalls, the Beatrice, Nebraska sheriff's office told him the Rulo farm was, in fact, a Posse training camp. In his travels during the winter, Whelan ran across Bob Lange, an ABC producer for the television news show *20/20*, who was himself crisscrossing the Midwest gathering material for a report on the far right. Lange showed the detective a copy of a May 1984 statement by a man named Donald Zabawa, who displayed considerable knowledge about the inner workings of the Posse. Zabawa, who had been arrested by Kansas authorities on charges of threatening a sheriff, made a lengthy confession to the KBI as part of an attempted plea bargain. The statement was later made public by the Ottawa County, Kansas district attorney.

The Zabawa statement was a hair-raising document that seemed to come from another planet. In it, Zabawa describes an elaborate network of groups and individuals operating under the political apparatus of the Posse and engaging in crime as a business. On the surface, it sounded like something out of the Wild West, weaving together such bizarre, apocalyptic organizations as the Posse; the Farmers Liberation Army; the Christian Patriots Defense League; and the Covenant, Sword & the Arm of the Lord. Zabawa told of plans to rob

The Zabawa Statement

[Donald Zabawa, who had been involved in the Posse Comitatus, made a statement to the Kansas Bureau of Investigation in 1984 as part of a failed plea bargain attempt. The statement, later recanted, gave authorities, for the first time, a detailed understanding of the inner workings of the Posse.]

I have heard that they were planning a base camp at * * *'s, but nothing has been done yet. . . .

Wickstrom and I discussed my case in general, and things in general. He said to arm myself and prepare for the "war" between the Posse and the system. He said the main battle would occur in Kansas. He said I should arm myself. He said the "movement" (Posse and all the Identity Christians) are going to overthrow the government (all government—U.S., Kansas, etc.) by force. He didn't say how or when. . . .

Some time in March 1984, I was sitting at the table in * * *'s house when he showed me a stack about 1½ inches high of letterhead paper entitled "The Committee to save the Judges from Hanging." He also had a bunch of envelopes with the same title. * * * said he had sent a letter to Judge * * * and signed it "The Chairman." He said he had a special typewriter just for such things that was not at his house. He said the typewriter was saved just for such things. . . .

* * * has made pipe bombs and experimented with them . . . * * * had the makings of pipe bombs at his house until about a week ago. He became worried about * * * being an officer or a snitch. He said * * * had money to buy guns and he didn't want to get involved in anything. As recently as three weeks ago * * * told me he was planning to blow up the unoccupied patrol car of the * * * Police Chief. He was going to do it because the city cops were hassling him. He didn't do anything about it. I talked about blowing up Deputy * * *'s car, at the County Sheriff's Office. I never did anything about it. . . .

a Federal Reserve Bank, to develop potent poisons, and to send court officers "practical joke" letters under letterhead reading, "The Committee to Save the Judges from Hanging." He quotes one man who nonchalantly lumps together his enemies as "Jews, cops, judges, lawyers — and everyone else who doesn't agree with him." Throughout, Zabawa recites a litany of crimes: stealing farm machinery, robbing gun dealers and restaurants, stealing police scanners. And he says that "Michael Ryan is Jim Wickstrom's man in Kansas . . . I went up to Ryan's house once. He wanted to know if I could get any weapons. He showed me two AR-15s that he said had been converted to fully automatic. . . . He said he had some M-60 machine guns. . . . Behind the TV, a section of the wall comes out which is where he stores some of his weapons. He said he keeps a lot of weapons at Rick Stice's [who was still living on the Rulo farm], his base camp. Ryan's group has vowed not to be taken alive."

"They don't believe in a lot of paperwork," the Zabawa statement continues. "They just want to kill Jews, people against the movement. . . . [One of Ryan's friends] has told me Ryan's group steals machinery and cattle from farmers and sells them. I don't know to who or where."

When the plea bargain failed and Zabawa went to prison, he recanted the statement. But for Whelan and the others in the network of researchers who were tracking the far right, the Zabawa statement was a gold mine of information, confirming relationships previously only suspected. Whelan distributed copies of the Zabawa statement to law enforcement officials across the farm belt, trying to interest them in the Posse and in trading information. He got nowhere.

As it turned out, law enforcement officials in Kansas already suspected Ryan of committing crimes

Aerial photo of the Rulo farm in Nebraska, taken in August of 1985 after a raid by an FBI SWAT team.

on two different occasions. KBI reports named Ryan in connection with an alleged 1982 theft of rifles from a store in Anthony, Kansas, and with the mailing of Posse literature to Kansas judges in 1983.

Because the Brown County, Kansas district attorney had represented Cheryl Gibson's parents on personal matters, the county appointed another local attorney, Pam Fahey, as a special prosecutor in the Cheryl Gibson case. In January 1985, Fahey went to Topeka to get some help from federal officials. She met with both an FBI agent and an assistant U.S. attorney, telling them about Cheryl's possible involvement with the Posse and asking for a federal flight warrant. Both officials refused on grounds that in this domestic dispute one of the parents was with the children, thereby assuring their safety. Like the sheriff of Brown County, they didn't want to get into a domestic dispute.

As for the Posse's involvement, the U.S. attorney later said he could not recall Fahey mentioning that possibility. Actually, in November, two months before Fahey met with the federal officials, the Kansas Bureau of Investigation had put out a "WANTED" bulletin for Cheryl and the children which read, "She is associated with the Posse Comitatus Group, who are believed to be helping her conceal the children."

In her efforts to find Cheryl, Fahey obtained the telephone records of Cheryl's parents and passed them along to Whelan, who found calls to Posse numbers in Wisconsin. Later, a Wickstrom lieutenant was arrested in Kansas, and the county attorney gave Whelan a copy of his address book. More names and addresses. Whelan used these to double check and expand on the information in the Zabawa statement.

By March 1985 Whelan was sure of the accuracy of much of the Zabawa statement, and was convinced that the Rulo farm was a Posse camp. But he was broke, and had to quit the case. Whelan's last suggestion before he quit, however, was to say that if Lester Gibson really wanted his children back, Whelan should be allowed to kidnap James Haverkamp, Cheryl's brother, and then exchange him for the children. But Lester Gibson would have none of it. "He did not want to break the law," Whelan recalled. "He believed so strongly in the law, and he thought eventually law enforcement agencies would help him. Every time we got

NEBRASKA STATE PATROL

Bunkhouse at the Rulo farm, Nebraska, after the raid.

any information he'd call them all up and give it to them. He never, until the very end, was convinced that these people were not going to help him."

Finally, in June of that year, the case unexpectedly broke. Late one night Kansas authorities near the Nebraska border spotted a group of men transferring what looked to be farm equipment from one truck to another. Suspicious, they radioed ahead to Nebraska. Richardson County Sheriff Cory McNabb — the man who took over when Sheriff Ramer died of cancer — saw a truck without any lights on towing a crop sprayer. He pulled it over and arrested two men — James Haverkamp and John David Andreas, both from the Rulo farm and both well-armed.

Shortly thereafter, McNabb and the Nebraska state patrol raided the Rulo property and found five truckloads of stolen farm machinery, more than thirty semiautomatic and assault rifles, thirteen fully automatic pistols and rifles, a sawed-off shotgun, camouflage gear, 150,000 rounds of ammunition, and at least one bunker stocked with food and water and its own electrical system. They also found quantities of Christian Identity and Posse literature, along with tapes of Jim Wickstrom. "We were really surprised," said Dan Scott of the Nebraska State Patrol. "I didn't expect to run into this much stuff."

This was more than a little disingenuous, since the state police had certainly known of the Zabawa confession, which described the Rulo farm as a "base camp" and named James Haverkamp as the one who stole farm machinery. After the raid, the Nebraska authorities picked up Mike Ryan and charged him with illegally possessing a machine gun.

On the evening of the Rulo raid, two Brown County deputies who had participated called Ted Collins, Lester Gibson's attorney, to tell him that both Cheryl and the kids were on the farm — and that Sheriff McNabb had refused to pick them up. Collins now got on the phone to try once more to persuade the county prosecutor, Douglas Merz, to arrest Cheryl and take the children into custody.

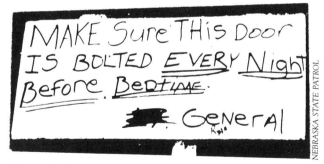

Placard nailed above Rulo farm door, and signed by "General Ryan."

But just as he had a year before, Merz refused to act on the Kansas warrants. In frustration, Collins sought out a local judge, who remonstrated with Merz. Still, Merz refused to act on the Kansas warrants. Collins then rounded up a local Nebraska attorney, who arranged a hearing with the judge, this time ordering Merz to exercise the warrants. By that evening, the children were turned over to Kansas authorities at the state line and transported to foster homes, where they remain. Meanwhile, Sheriff McNabb picked up Cheryl Gibson — but instead of taking her to jail, he drove her to an attorney. Bail was speedily arranged, and she returned to the farm.

When Pam Fahey, still the special prosecutor in Brown County, called McNabb and said she wanted him to extradite Cheryl, McNabb got angry and hung up.

Over the course of the year, Merz and McNabb not only balked repeatedly at pursuing outstanding Kansas felony warrants, but also played down other aspects of the Rulo raid, which had turned up large caches of ammunition, guns, and Posse literature. "I have no idea what their affiliations are," county prosecutor Merz told the *Kansas City Times* after the first raid, referring to the group living at the farm. "At present there is no evidence to indicate what they are, except that they had quite a few automatic weapons and a lot of ammunition."

Even after the raid, McNabb continued to maintain friendly contact with the people on the Rulo farm. In fact, a few days after the raid he drove National Public Radio's Frank Browning and another reporter to the farm, where he climbed out of his cruiser and walked up to the farmhouse to set up an interview. Fifteen minutes later he emerged, followed by Mike Ryan and Cheryl Gibson. Browning proceeded to interview the two across the farm gate. When he asked Cheryl where her kids went to school, McNabb broke in. "Well, you turn that thing off," Browning recalls the sheriff saying, pointing at the tape recorder. "I wouldn't want Cheryl to get in trouble just because I'm good enough to let you come out here." And before television cameras, Mike Ryan was highly complimentary of McNabb. "I think Richardson County has elected themselves a fine sheriff," he said, "and they ought to keep him."

On Saturday, August 17, McNabb appeared at the Rulo farm once again, and while the details of what happened have never been clear, he apparently persuaded Ryan, Cheryl Gibson, and her cousin Timothy Haverkamp to come back into town with him. Once in town, Ryan and Haverkamp were both seized by lawmen and held, as a search party of eighty lawmen, including an FBI SWAT team, entered the property, proceeded to a clearing past the main houses, and began to dig. Soon they had unearthed two bodies, one a decomposed corpse of a young boy, the other that of a man in his twenties.

Why the Rulo town attorney and sheriff refused to intervene in the affairs of the farm before state and federal authorities entered the case has never been explained. Had they acted on Lester Gibson's earlier requests, lives might have been saved. At the trial it was revealed that Ryan had murdered the five-year-old boy because they thought he was a "mongrel," the child's mother supposedly having had sex with an "Indian." Ryan and a group of men on the farm had participated in killing the

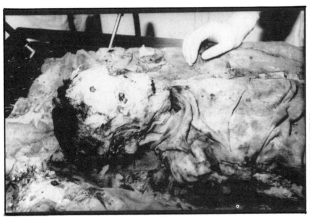

Corpse, dug up by the FBI on the Rulo farm, of a five-year-old boy murdered by Posse Comitatus leader Mike Ryan.

young man, a member of Ryan's Posse group, by taking him out to a hog shed, chaining him to a post, and slowly inserting a shovel handle into his anus until the handle pierced his intestine. Other tortures had included kicking him, punching him, shooting off his fingers and skinning him while he was still alive; and a *coup de grace* had been administered with a pistol shot into the head. This young man's crime had been to challenge Ryan's godly authority. Ryan was found guilty of murder and sentenced to die. He is now on death row in the Nebraska state prison in Lincoln, rewriting the Bible according to the dictates of Christian Identity.

New
White
Politics

CHAPTER 5

New White Politics

"Traitors there in parliament, bought off by the Jews / Nationalist Opposition is only bound to lose," go the lines to "Bloodsucker," performed by the British far-right skin band No Remorse. "Reject their corrupt system, stand now for your race/Cos when we finally win, they will have no place."

By the late 1980s, the far right in the United States had begun to forge ties with similar groups abroad. This progress toward an international movement was achieved at first by skinheads, who also struck up an alliance in the United States with the Ku Klux Klan. In addition to the birth of this street-fighting youth movement, the far right began, in the eighties, to move successfully into electoral politics. At the head of these new incarnations of far-right activity were two former Klansmen.

David Duke of Louisiana and his former California lieutenant, Tom Metzger, offered new hope for a white revolution. Duke emerged as the resilient leader of a political movement with the potential for widespread popularity and power. Metzger set out to create a street-fighting army by recruiting racist skinheads into the Klan. Duke and Metzger have seen the Fifth Era, and it shows signs of working.

Whistling Dixie with Duke

Born in Tulsa, Oklahoma and educated at a private military school in Georgia, the young David Duke was an avid reader, and by age thirteen he was well on his way to becoming a liberal. But reading Carlton Putnam's *Race and Reason*, which questioned integration, touched something dark and funky in Duke's makeup, and by the age of seventeen he had joined the Klan.

Duke attended Louisiana State University, and there, in 1969, he formed the White Youth Alliance, which ultimately became the National Party. It did little more than hand out Duke's leaflets. Dressed up as a storm trooper, Duke picketed William Kunstler, attorney for the Chicago Seven. During a local radio program, he argued that Jews should be exterminated and blacks sent back to Africa. *Reveille*, the Tulane University student newspaper, quoted Duke saying, "I am a National Socialist. You can call me a Nazi if you want." By 1970, Duke was writing, "The plain truth is our race is losing. We're losing our schools to Black savagery, losing our hard-earned pay to Black welfare, losing our lives to No-Win Red treason and Black crime, losing our culture to Jewish and Black degeneracy, and we are losing our most precious possession, our white racial heritage, to race-mixing."

In 1975, Duke formed his own Knights of the Ku Klux Klan in Louisiana, transforming them from rednecks in sheets to good ol' boys in wing-tip shoes.

For all of Duke's evident success at projecting the new image of the buttoned-down Klan, there were glimmers of other sides to his personality. Under a pseudonym, he wrote *Finders Keepers*, a manual for women who were trying to get a man, providing sex tips along with advice on makeup.

Then, under the name Mohammed X, he wrote *African Atto*, a street-fighting manual for blacks to help them in their battles with white oppressors. It contains elaborate descriptions of martial arts kicks and punches that might be aimed at "whitey." Mohammed X suggests that whenever confronting the white man, blacks should yell out "hootoo" to frighten him, not to mention "rid the body of bad air."

Duke's grandstanding style and popularity seeking ways made enemies among his fellow Klansmen. One of them, Karl Hand, was a longtime intimate of Duke, a national organizer of the Louisiana Knights of the Ku Klux Klan, and later the commanding officer of the National Socialist Liberation Front. (He went to prison for attempted murder.) In his newspaper, Hand accused Duke of "conduct unbecoming a racist," and wrote, "The list here is almost endless, but let's leave it at this. . . . Don't leave your wife, your girl friend or your daughters alone with this guy. He has the morals of a jew. This ego manical [*sic*] displays have cost Duke many a member. I can't tell you how many people used to call up KKK headquarters to complain about the Grand Wizard's behavior."

In 1980, Duke ally Bill Wilkinson left the Knights to set up his own competing Invisible Empire. The identity of a Klansman is supposed to be a tightly kept secret, and membership lists are therefore guarded by the leadership as if they were the Ark of the Covenant. Nonetheless, Wilkinson was able to persuade Duke to violate his Klan oath and sell the membership list of the Knights of the KKK for $35,000. Wilkinson secretly videotaped Duke making the deal. He then threatened to play the videotape for a Klan membership meeting. Soon thereafter, Duke quit the Klan, leaving it in the hands of his friend Don Black, another new-style Klansman who would

Knights of the Ku Klux Klan leader David Duke poses in his Klan robe during a recruiting trip to London in 1978.

later marry Duke's ex-wife. The final chapter in this sordid saga came when Klansmen later discovered that Wizard Wilkinson himself had been an FBI informer since 1974.

After bailing out of the Klan in 1980, Duke started yet another organization, this one called the National Association for the Advancement of White People (NAAWP), whose purpose was to promote racial separatism. Duke eschewed the styles and tactics of aggressive white supremacy, and adopted the persona of the boyishly good-looking white civil rights activist. "The ultimate answer to this racial quagmire is racial separatism," said the *NAAWP News*. "The Jews, blacks, Hispanics and Orientals would each be given a portion of the present-day United States so they could have a nation of their own. The rest of America would be reserved for the white majority."

Under this plan, originally published in the right-wing magazine *Instauration* and later reprinted in the December 1984 *NAAWP News*, blacks could live in a New Africa made up of parts of Georgia, Alabama, and Mississippi. Jews would dwell in West Israel, comprised of Long Island and Manhattan, while the remainder of the New York metropolitan area and southern Connecticut would be home to various "unassimilable minorities," including Puerto Ricans, southern Italians, Greeks, and immigrants from the southern Mediterranean littoral. Mexicans would get the Southwest, except for a slice of territory called Navahona, which would be reserved for American Indians. The Hawaiian Islands would be called East Mongolia, set aside for Asians. Dade County, Florida would be the New Cuba. Anyone straying across the borders of their new countries would be shot on sight. White America would also establish all-white outposts in space. And under a eugenics program, the whites would grow into a dreamy race of Aryan supermen,

blond-haired, blue-eyed, with an average I.Q. of 144. Duke proposed awarding whites with high I.Q.s government loans that they could repay by having genetically superior children.

Duke warned that without such measures, the white race would be overrun by the "nonwhite world." In 1983 in the NAAWP newsletter, he wrote:

> Immigration . . . along with nonwhite birthrates will make white people a minority totally vulnerable to the political, social, and economic will of blacks, Mexicans, Puerto Ricans, and Orientals. A social upheaval is now beginning to occur that will be the funeral dirge of the America we love. I shudder to contemplate the future under nonwhite occupation; rapes, murders, robberies multiplied a hundred fold, illiteracy such as in Haiti, medicine such as in Mexico, and tyranny such as in Togoland. Am I an alarmist? Is my vision unreal? All one has to do is look around this globe and see the Third World reality. Are whites holding every one of the nonwhite countries down, or are we in fact pumping billions of dollars into them along with every technological aid that the West can produce? And now the West itself is gradually being enveloped by nonwhite immigration. The exploding numbers of nonwhites are slowly wrapping formerly white nations in a dark human cocoon. Shall a butterfly emerge, or a beast that has haunted the ruins of every great white civilization that submitted to invasion by immigration and racial miscegenation?

Not everyone thought David Duke was the epitome of white power. Some thought he was a flim-flam man, others viewed him as a spook. Those who thought he was an agent cited as evidence the fact that he claimed to have served a short stint in 1971 in Vientiane, Laos, where the CIA was running its secret air war. He has told reporters of teaching English to anticommunist officers under the auspices of the U.S. AID program. Patsy Sims, who has written a detailed ac-

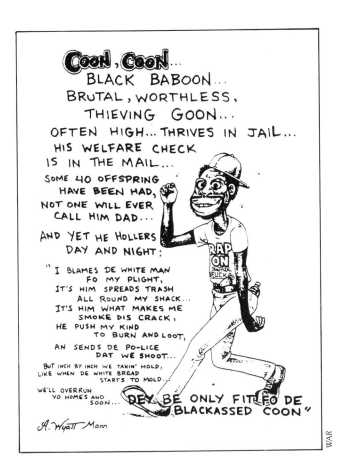

of Dominica to restore that country's right-wing premier. Black was sent to jail for three years. In an interview with the Associated Press, Duke said the Dominica coup effort was the first step in a covert action which, he claimed, had the support of the CIA and was aimed at wresting control of Grenada from leftist Maurice Bishop and restoring Sir Eric Gairy. Duke was called before a grand jury investigating the Dominica excursion, but later insisted that he had not answered any questions. And he said the Klan's only role in the operation was recruiting men willing to join the mercenary force.

Whatever he was doing covertly, David Duke's real contribution to the far right was quite overt. Making use of a "tripartisan strategy," Duke set out in 1988 to run for president of the United States. Duke began as a Democrat in the southern primaries. Running in the general election on the third-party ticket of the far-right Populist Party, Duke gained maximum visibility in Louisiana, where he won 23,000 votes. He was then in a good position to switch to the Republican Party. In 1989, as a Republican, Duke ran for the Louisiana state legislature, representing the New Orleans suburb of Metairie. Mining the same lode of white, worried, middle-class voters, he edged out his opponent, John Treen, who had the support of both Ronald Reagan and George Bush, and propelled the racialist movement into the heart of mainstream two-party politics.

Although Duke said in 1988 that he had cut all ties to the Klan and other white power groups, there was every indication that the KKK and white resistance leaders were at the forefront of his presidential campaign. In early 1987, Duke was a featured speaker at the Klan rally in Forsyth County, Georgia, the scene of several white power demonstrations that year. There Duke helped local Klans-

count of Duke's life in her book *The Klan*, wondered, along with Louisiana cops and some Klansmen, whether he was an intelligence agent. When Sims confronted him with Klan accusations that he was a secret agent, Duke scoffed.

But the possibility of a covert connection gained credence in the early 1980s, when Duke's friend Don Black and eight other racists, all members of the Klan or neo-Nazi groups, were arrested by the FBI at a Louisiana marina. They had been preparing to launch a coup on the Caribbean island

The National Premise
A Proposed Geographical Relocation and Regrouping of America's Unassimilable Minorities

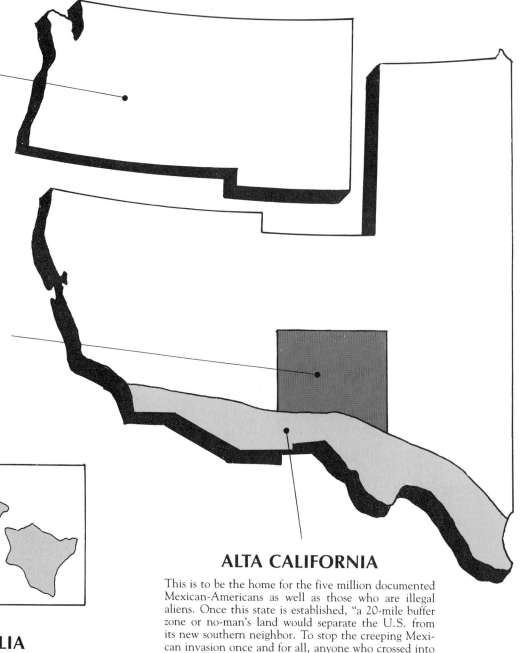

THE WHITE BASTION*

This area — made up of Washington, Oregon, Montana, Wyoming, and Idaho — is the proposed homeland for racists. This plan is the brainchild of Robert Miles as well as other members of the Aryan Nations.

> *"The White Bastion" is not part of the David Duke blueprint, but represents the preference of some Aryan Nations members to form an all-white enclave.*

NAVAHONA

This will be the permanent home for 800,000 American Indians. "Although the land is not rich or fertile . . . there is no reason why Indians . . . will not have enough elbow room, once the whites have decamped."

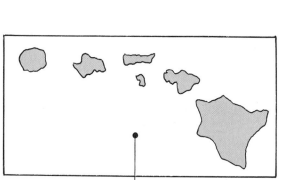

EAST MONGOLIA

The Hawaiian Islands would become the home for all Chinese, Japanese, Filipino, and other Orientals currently living in Hawaii and the mainland U.S. Though not specifically mentioned, presumably native Hawaiians will be permitted to live in East Mongolia.

ALTA CALIFORNIA

This is to be the home for the five million documented Mexican-Americans as well as those who are illegal aliens. Once this state is established, "a 20-mile buffer zone or no-man's land would separate the U.S. from its new southern neighbor. To stop the creeping Mexican invasion once and for all, anyone who crossed into this buffer zone without permission from both countries will be shot on sight."

A version of this map of a radically segregated United States* was featured in the December 1984 issue of David Duke's *NAAWP News*. The architects of this plan recognize that while some of the relocations might be difficult, there have been historical instances where large numbers of people have been displaced, such as "the 6 million Americans sent overseas in World War II and the 11 million Germans who fled from the Russians in 1945 —not to mention the 3.5 million Palestinians displaced by the Jews" in the Middle East.

FRANCIA

The proposed "independent state of America's 3 million French-Canadians who, although assimilable in a physical and cultural sense, will probably never be able to escape the emotional pull of their homeland."

MINORIA

The rest of the New York metropolitan area (less Manhattan and Long Island) is set aside for Puerto Ricans, southern Italians, Greeks, immigrants from the eastern and southern regions of the Mediterranean, and other "unassimilable minorities." Each of these groups is expected to live and work within its respective enclave.

WEST ISRAEL

This new state — located in what is currently Long Island and Manhattan — is to contain the entire Jewish population of the United States. "Jews from the Bronx, Westchester and other New York suburbs will only have a short move . . . as will those from Boston, Philadelphia, and Washington, D.C. Migrants from Miami Beach, Chicago and Los Angeles will have greater difficulty relocating." It is noted that at least four million non-Jews will have to leave West Israel to make room for the Jews.

NEW AFRICA

"Almost 12 million Negroes will have to be transported from northern urban centers, and millions of southern Negroes will have to be regrouped" within this new state. "Whites . . . will probably not give up their homes peacefully. In Florida, however, where hardly anyone has roots, population transfers will be easier."

NEW CUBA

What is now Miami, Miami Beach and Dade County is reserved for the 600,000 Cuban-Americans. "Only Negroes, Jews and a few aged Majority members will have to vacate."

David Duke as Imperial Wizard of the Knights of the Ku Klux Klan looking for illegal aliens along the California/Mexico border in 1977.

men establish an anti-black organization called the Forsyth County Defense League. Klan leaders from across the country attended his presidential campaign kickoff meeting in June of 1987 near Marietta, Georgia.

The campaign manager of Duke's 1988 presidential bid was Ralph P. Forbes, who had been the western U.S. commander of George Lincoln Rockwell's American Nazi Party during the 1960s. By 1988 Forbes was the pastor at the Sword of Christ Good News Ministries in London, Arkansas, where he called himself "chaplain at large of God's White Army." In 1986, Forbes made an unsuccessful race for lieutenant governor in Arkansas, where, he later told the *New Orleans Times-Picayune*, "I was known as the Nazi candidate." (In 1990, Forbes

was to run again, this time scoring an upset victory as a Republican in the first round before being swamped in the run-off.) In his presidential bid, Duke had support not only from the Klan, but also from Willis Carto's Liberty Lobby, whose newspaper, the *Spotlight*, pumped up Duke on a regular basis.

During his 1989 campaign for the Louisiana state legislature, the national Republican Party took pains to disassociate itself from Duke. Ronald Reagan cut a radio spot in support of his opponent, and Bush sent in his son George, who delivered a prep-schoolish defense of Duke's opponent. Duke himself continued to play his racist lines, introducing himself at meeting after meeting as a "former" Ku Klux Klansman. He ran against taxes and af-

THE NEW YORK TIMES **NATIONAL** *MONDAY, JUNE 18, 1990*

Ex-Klansman Puts New Racial Politics to Test

By PETER APPLEBOME

Special to The New York Times

FRANKLIN, La. — It's racial politics for the 90's — not Old South race baiting, but a post-civil-rights-era assault on welfare abuse and programs like affirmative action that his audience sees as helping blacks while hurting whites.

"I'm not a racist like Jesse Jackson," David Duke said recently, peering into the Cajun country blue-collar crowd of perhaps 200 people at the American Legion hall here. "I'm proud of my heritage like Jesse Jackson is proud of his. But I believe the time has come for equal rights for everyone in this country, even for white people."

Many in the crowd wear blue and
   David Duke T-shirts or baseball

caps, and they give their approval in a low rumble of "Duke, Duke, Duke, Duke," a response that has made the roadshow of the former Ku Klux Klan leader the talk of Louisiana.

A year after his surprise election to the Louisiana House of Representatives, Mr. Duke has made himself a po-

tent force in state politics, polarizing the Legislature along racial lines, gathering a fervent statewide following and mounting an unexpectedly strong bid for the United States Senate seat held by J. Bennett Johnston.

Despite the enthusiastic crowds, analysts say there is little chance he can

firmative action. The sudden and well-publicized appearance of Mordecai Levy, the head of the Jewish Defense Organization, in New Orleans as the campaign entered its critical phase may have helped Duke.

Duke's campaign survived two censure attempts, a radio blitz, and the appeals from Ronald Reagan. On his swearing in, the legislature rose to give the new representative from Metairie a standing ovation.

Once in office, Duke proposed several different bills. One of them would have required drug tests for recipients of public assistance, including food stamps and Medicaid. By adding such requirements, which were not included in federal legislation, the state probably would have forfeited the $1.5 billion in federal money it was receiving each year. Other Duke bills would have increased penalties for drug offenses in public housing, required drug tests for first-time teenage drivers, and ended affirmative action and minority set-aside programs. In May of 1990, against all predictions, a Duke-sponsored anti-affirmative action bill passed in the Louisiana House. Even if passed in both houses, all of Duke's proposed legislation would be of dubious constitutionality; but it put a legislative face on Duke's smoothed-out racism.

While Duke's legislative program was stymied, he himself quickly proved to be a resilient politician. National Republican chairman Lee Atwater called Duke a "charlatan" with "no place in the party," and made efforts to censure him; but Atwater was rebuffed by the state Republican leaders. Later, efforts were made by moderate Louisiana party members to pass their own censure motion. Duke presented many Louisiana Republicans with an especially embarrassing problem. One third of the members of the party's central committee were evangelical Christians who strongly supported Is-

rael. "I consider myself to have a Jewish heart," Neil Curran, a media consultant and member of the committee declared. "I had a personal experience with a Jewish person who changed my life: Jesus Christ. Jews are God's chosen people. Party leadership needs to know Duke's real positions — his anti-Semitism, his great love for Hitler and Nazi writings. I think it's impossible for someone who is truly an evangelical to support David Duke." But other members did not agree, and the censure motion failed.

Although Duke might have seemed to have moderated his political views, his ideas were virtually unchanged. Shortly after his election he went to Chicago to address a Populist Party meeting, and was quickly attacked in the press for shaking hands with a Nazi Party leader. Tulane University researchers discovered he was promoting and selling Nazi, racist, and anti-Semitic literature from the basement of his legislative office in Metairie. His staff included Trish Katzen, who had previously worked at the Liberty Lobby office in Washington on behalf of the Populist Party. And in a lengthy interview with Tulane student Abby Kaplan, in November 1989, Duke elaborated on his hopes for a white Aryan society:

I wouldn't say Hitler was right on race, but I do believe that there are genetic differences between races and that they profoundly affect culture. . . . I think that for instance there's differences in physical abilities, there's differences in musical abilities, there's differences in I.Q. . . . The top 16 finalists for the 100 meter dash at the Olympics . . . last year were all black. But there's no prohibition against whites running the 100 meter dash. I mean there's something genetic that gives them an advantage in that particular contest. There's some things that give whites advantages in certain areas. And I.Q. is a reflection of western culture . . . I.Q. is pretty much a reflection of how well someone will do in school. It has

David Duke is cheered by supporters after winning a seat in the Louisiana House of Representatives in 1989.

been an accurate predictor. And I think whites score better in that particular category, that particular talent. It doesn't mean they are innately superior, but it's a mistake, and it's kind of unfair to say that, well, because you agree with some aspects of Germany, therefore you're a Nazi.

Asked whether he thought it was a mistake for the U.S. to have entered World War II, Duke replied:

> I think that we should not have gotten involved in the war. I think that the war cost tens of millions of lives — including the Holocaust. . . . I agree with George Patton . . . I think that the Second World War has been a disaster. It gave half of Europe to the communists which we're finally now beginning to alleviate. It threw half of the world into communist slavery, so I don't think the war was really fought over freedom . . . how in the world are we fighting for freedom when our allies are the greatest mass murderers of all time — the Soviets. You know, they didn't kill six million. The Soviet Union killed 66 million. . . . So yeh, I think the Second World War was damaging to the West and to freedom, even though I don't agree with National Socialist philosophy.

When Kaplan asked Duke whether he thought his proposal for rewarding people with high I.Q.'s government loans in order to have children conflicted with equal rights, Duke said, "I don't think it does at all. Right now the government is doing that in reverse. The low-income, low I.Q. people [who] are least able to function in our society have the highest birthrates in our society. And so government is encouraging the least capable and least talented people that have the highest birthrate. I think that's disastrous. . . . That's against evolution."

In 1990 Duke declared his bid to unseat U.S. Senator J. Bennett Johnston, the Democratic incumbent who had held the seat for three terms.

Dismissed at first as a joke, Duke won grudging acceptance among political pros as he pulled big crowds who cheered his attacks on welfare chisellers and his opposition to raising taxes. By spring, Duke was polling 25 percent to Johnston's 65 percent. More importantly, Duke was able to pile up campaign contributions and develop a national base of support through direct mail. By late spring he had raised more than $700,000 with direct-mail attacks on Johnston for siding with the "ultra liberal Ted Kennedy" and "the policies of Jesse Jackson," and for voting against defeated Supreme Court nominee Robert Bork because Johnston feared the "black bloc vote." Duke also had amassed a list of more than 30,000 national donors, most of them making donations of about twenty-five dollars each.

Duke's Senate campaign was an amalgam of his old Klan line: bashing welfare cheats, cracking down on crime, changing the welfare system — all issues subtly linked to blacks and other minorities. But this kinder, gentler racism was wrapped in pseudo-populist rhetoric: denunciations of companies that pollute the environment and don't pay taxes, attacks on special interest groups, assaults on the Japanese for buying American companies, and calls for higher tariffs on foreign goods. At rallies, most Duke supporters were white, often in their late middle age, who did not consider themselves racists. "I feel like we're being walked on," one of these Duke supporters told the *New Orleans Times-Picayune*. "We have to stand up for our rights. They shouldn't get an edge. But I'm not anti-black."

Bo Ackal, the Democratic state representative from New Iberia, explained Duke's appeal in a newspaper interview early in the campaign: "He's really appealing to the young people on the college campuses and the young workers. They feel they've been discriminated against. They're frustrated. They can't get jobs or they see their fathers working, struggling to put them through school, and they think it's all being handed to blacks because of race." These younger voters do not identify themselves with problems of age-old discrimination suffered by blacks, but they do believe they are being asked to suffer because of that prior discrimination.

Tomorrow Belongs to Me

In the spring of 1989, recruiting posters for the Invisible Empire of the Ku Klux Klan appeared on the streets of Edinburgh, Scotland. Soon thereafter James W. Farrands, the grand wizard of the Invisible Empire, travelled to England to recruit

National Front

members in Scotland and Wales, and from among the British military. *Searchlight*, the British magazine that carries on a close scrutiny of the right in Europe, later reported that the Invisible Empire had inducted 400 British members into the Klan at a secret ceremony in Wales. Farrands himself later agreed that *Searchlight* "was estimating fairly good." He went on to explain that the Invisible Empire was recruiting in France, Belgium, West Germany, Australia, Spain, Italy, and Scandinavia. This was the first such successful foray abroad since the early 1920s, when the Klan had established a klavern in Germany.

Farrands is a car mechanic who in 1990 moved the headquarters of the Invisible Empire from Connecticut to North Carolina, where he promised to jump into electoral politics. The Invisible Empire, which was launched in the 1970s by Bill Wilkinson as a split-off from David Duke's Louisiana Klan,

became one of the most aggressive and truculent racist groups in the nation. Its Virginia recruiter was John Walker, the U.S. Navy radio man who was convicted of selling secrets to the Russians. (Walker's recruiting activities coincided with a surge in Klan membership in the U.S. Navy, sparking reports of hooded mariners mysteriously rising up out of the hatchways to spook black seamen.) Founder Wilkinson came to grief in the early 1980s, when it was revealed that he had long been an FBI informant. This revelation led to mass resignations and the breakup of one of the largest and most obstreperous Klans in the post-war era. Yet it was this hangdog fragment of white power, the Invisible Empire, that the car mechanic from Connecticut sought to fashion into an international network.

Fortuitously for Farrands, his missionary work coincided with what appeared to be an international renaissance of the far right. In Western Europe, as in the United States, the far right breaks down into a two-tiered movement, consisting of respectable-sounding politicians on the one hand, and a rowdy youth movement on the other. In the past few years, advances have been made on both fronts in all the industrialized economies of the West.

On the face of it, Klan recruiting in Britain was a daunting prospect. The far right there has long been the province of the National Front, itself an amalgam of several different factions. The most important of these factions were the British National Party, a national socialist organization, and the League of Empire Loyalists, described by some as a group of far-out Tories and by others as anti-Semitic cranks. The National Front grew from a membership of 4,000 upon its founding in 1966 to 17,500 in 1973. The new members came from inner-city Labor constituencies, and from the ranks of Tories who thought Prime Minister Edward Heath was not sufficiently vigorous in supporting the white government in Rhodesia. In addition, they thought the Conservative leadership was lax on law-and-order issues, and especially on matters of immigration. But soon the members of the Front fell to squabbling over their internal goals, and then fell apart under the pressure of Margaret Thatcher's radical Toryism, which deflated the independent right. In the face of this dramatic loss of members and influence, the far right was ready to regroup, imitating the American experience.

Meanwhile, on the continent, the far right was reorganizing. In the late 1970s and early 1980s, there had been a wave of bombings in Germany, France, and Italy. In Italy these bombings took more than 100 lives, and were perpetrated by a terror group called the Armed Revolutionary Nuclei (NAR). "The suspicions voiced at the time, that [the bombings] were connected with the notorious P2 Freemasons' lodge and right-wing elements within state security, have now been confirmed by convictions in the Italian courts," *Searchlight* wrote in its lengthy reconstruction of the situation. In Europe, as in the U.S., many right-wing activities were financed by a series of robberies, in particular a bank heist in Spain.

In the early 1980s, European members of the far right began getting together to organize a liaison among different groups. At this point the British National Front was in the doldrums, its membership down to 4,000. After a bombing in Bologna the British Nazis were asked to provide safe housing for Italians on the run. When the Italians arrived, they were looking for a vehicle to accomplish a wider reorganization and seized upon the bankrupt National Front, essentially taking it over. They were soon joined by the Spanish bank robbers and, along with a British faction inside the National

Front, they then set out to create a new British-based movement. To this end, they further disbanded the National Front, shrinking its membership to about 1,000 die-hard supporters, from whose midst they could build a cadre, ready to sacrifice itself if need be. As plans evolved, they decided that in addition to the cadre there would be aboveground organizations that could flirt along the far-right edges of the Conservative Party and conduct the traditional baiting of blacks, Jews, and other people of color. Members of these aboveground groups could stand for election, hold demonstrations, and keep tabs on the growing skinhead movement, which was meant to serve as the street-fighting arm of the racialist right.

As this "political soldier" wing of the old National Front took shape, its leaders made contact with Libyan Colonel Qaddafi, various radical Iranian elements, and, in a crackpot move to capitalize on black nationalist sentiments, tried to strike up a relationship with Louis Farrakhan in the United States. The political soldier wing of the Front kept a tight grip on Ian Stuart Donaldson, leader of the popular skinhead band Skrewdriver, and his "White Noise" movement, raking in proceeds from sales of records, tapes, videos, badges, and T-shirts. It still influences the skinheads and, in general, dominates life on the British far right.

Across the channel, the French National Front, headed by Jean-Marie Le Pen, steadily gained prominence during the late 1980s, borne on a wave of anti-immigration fervor directed against North Africans. Le Pen himself gained his highest visibility during the presidential elections of 1988, when he scored 14 percent of the vote in the first round. Le Pen ran strongly opposed to immigration on the theme of "France for Frenchmen," and "Racism in France today means patriotism." Among his most startling comments was "Genocide in Nazi Germany was just a detail in history." Socialist leader François Mitterrand eventually won the election, but in the spring of 1990 a poll found that 18 percent of the respondents favored having Le Pen play an important role in France. Although the popularity of the National Front rises and falls, it has demonstrated impressive electoral strength in certain areas of the country. During the late 1980s it won 67 percent of the vote in Dreux, a town in Normandy, and 47 percent in the southern seaport of Marseille in parliamentary bi-elections. Le Pen had revived the myth of a Jewish world conspiracy, which he called the "Jewish Internationale." After the bi-election results were totalled, Le Pen launched a tirade against a Jewish cabinet minister, and suggested police should search the Sentier district of Paris, where many clothing firms have Jewish owners, in pursuit of illegal immi-

East German skinheads give the Nazi salute during a February 1990 demonstration in Leipzig.

grants. In addition, he proposed the mass expulsion of immigrants who had come into France since 1974.

In May 1990, after vandals desecrated more than thirty graves at the Jewish cemetery of Carpentras near Avignon in southern France, dragging corpses out of tombs and leaving the body of one old man impaled with an umbrella through the anus, Mitterrand's government sought to link Le Pen's party to the crime. "Anti-Semitism is only the most obvious sign of a return to fascistic ideas on which the National Front builds up its electoral business," said Henri Emmanuelli, the Socialist Party's secretary-general. Le Pen denied any connection, claiming the desecration of the cemetery was a "fake" to discredit his movement.

The situation in France was only the most blatant example of the revival of right-wing racialism. In West Germany, respectable politicians spoke loftily of such things as German values, a restoration of the national borders of 1937, the rightful place of women in the home, and the danger of unchecked immigration. In the 1988 West German elections, the far-right Republikaner Party (REP) won seats in city and local governments around the country, as well as a bloc of votes in the European parliament. In West Berlin the REP won eleven seats in the city's parliament. A few months later the National Democrats, an REP rival on the far right, won seven seats in the Frankfurt city parliament. Led by Franz Schonhuber, a former member of the Waffen SS, the REP won representation in several major cities, including Cologne, Dortmund, Stuttgart and Mannheim. One 1990 survey of West German attitudes towards Jews, quoted by *Newsweek* in May 1990, found that among people aged sixty to sixty-five, three out of ten were openly anti-Semitic — though only one in twenty young people felt the same

way. By 1990 the Republikaners pulled a steady 8 to 10 percent in the polls, and according to *Searchlight*, East German polls showed them pulling down 8 percent there as well. Despite the fact that the REP and other fascist organizations were banned outright in East Germany, support for the Repub-

likaners is strong among their skilled technical workers, including those in factories where the communists had once held sway. Skinheads first appeared in East Germany in 1988, and one estimate now places their numbers at 5,000 to 10,000. And in one year there were over 200 reported incidents of racist incitement.

As the Berlin Wall came down and revolution swept the communists from Eastern Europe, anti-Semitism, borne along on the currents of nationalism and religion, made a reappearance. In Hungary, which has yet to admit its role in the Holocaust, anti-Semites accused Jews of causing all their troubles. Jewish professionals, listening to their answering machines, would get messages that said things like, "Dirty stinking Jew, we'll send you back to Auschwitz." At soccer matches, the Budapest team MTK — which had been founded by Jews more than a century ago, and now has only gentile players — was regularly taunted by its rivals with chants of "No goals for the Jews. Dirty Jews, Jews, Jews. To the gas chambers, gas chambers, gas chambers." Budapest taxis refused to take passengers if the drivers thought them to be Jews. The Nazi-era fascist organization Arrow Cross made a reappearance. And Istvan Csurka, a leader of the Democratic Forum, the opposition party which won a majority in the spring elections, has claimed "those Jews who have now lost power are stirring up trouble."

Like the Hungarians, the newly liberated Romanians, who had hung Jews up on hooks during the Second World War under signs that read "Kosher Meat," began blaming Jews for all their problems. And in Poland, where the entire Jewish population was wiped out in the Holocaust, politicians of the far right embarked upon a bizarre witch hunt for Jews in the Solidarity movement.

In the Soviet Union, the ultra-nationalist

WAR

Pamyat and other rightist groups rediscovered the *Protocols*, arguing, just as the Czar's secret police would have hoped a hundred years ago, that Jews not only killed Christ and the Czar, but also organized the Bolshevik revolution and ran Stalin's terror campaigns. (In fact, few Jews were ever admitted to the Communist Party hierarchy in the Soviet Union.) *Perestroika* and *glasnost* were depicted as part of a conspiracy to allow Jewish capitalists to control the country.

By the spring of 1990 the nationalist movements within the Soviet Union had begun to exercise an increasingly powerful role in politics, with the European parts of the nation — Russia, Byelorussia, the Baltic states, and the Ukraine — growing closer together and seeing themselves arrayed against what many believed to be the less "civilized," backward republics of central Asia. What was politely described as ethnic rivalry posed a long-term divisive factor in internal Soviet politics. With the rise of a revolutionary Moslem fundamentalism in Azerbaijan, the Soviet Union faced its Ulster. Within Russia itself, the nationalist movement was an important force in the environmental movement that was fast becoming a driving political force. And the rise of Russian nationalism reverberated with the question of racialism.

The "respectable" rightists are complemented by a far more potent — and more intimidating — group of youthful recruits coalesced around the skinhead movement. All across Western Europe, the ranks of poorly educated, unemployed white youth are growing. Finding its voice in quickly duplicated skinhead fanzines, the skin movement stretches from Britain across Germany, Poland, and Hungary, and into the Soviet Union itself. Its

Skinheads in Birmingham, England, in 1980.

members have few political pretensions, nor, for that matter, any serious political interests. They are more than content with a go at bashing Turks, Pakistanis, and other minorities. But, "If you put these together with older people who have grown up in the Klan or the American Nazi Party or whatever," remarked Jerry Gable, *Searchlight*'s publisher, "and if the older people start to pull the strings, then you've got a very effective army of kids around who are extremely violent."

The fact that the Nazi skinheads have become the shock troops of the rightist resurgence in Europe as well as in America over the past five years or so is a historical irony of loopy proportions. When bands of male teenagers — all wearing high-laced work boots, suspenders, short or rolled-cuff jeans, and plaid shirts, their hair shaved close to the skull — began appearing in London streets in the late 1960s, they were actually identified *with* black culture. Skins were at first considered a splinter of the Mods, a fashion culture that dominated the rock 'n' roll society of the time. The Mods, like the New Wavers of the early 1980s, carried neatness and apparent conformity to the point of absurdity — a Mod would wear a necktie like any businessman, but it would be too narrow to be quite *normal*. The inspiration for their dandyism lay in black culture. Mods saw black men like James Brown and Smokey Robinson as more than outposts of Soul — they were viewed as men who had escaped their class, wise to their irredeemably low status within society, but somehow able to outwit their betters by enjoying life more intensely.

In the late 1960s and the early 1970s, one group of Mods veered into hippiedom; another, the 'hard Mods,' sporting heavy boots, jeans, and short hair, turned away from acid rock and got into ska, rocksteady, and reggae. Where the Mods had been upwardly mobile, the skins, dressed as a "kind

of caricature of the model worker," explored the lumpen proletariat, creating a fused identity out of the culture of West Indian immigrants and the white working class. A hallmark of this new subculture was early eighties Brit rock — multiracial bands singing reggae songs about "rude boys" (Jamaican slang for delinquents) to overwhelmingly white audiences. "Superimposed one on top of the other, these two very different traditions coalesced around the skinheads' visual style, which simultaneously embodied both: the clean-cut, neatly pressed delinquent look owed at least as much to the rude boys as it did to the 'formalized and very "hard" stereotypes of the white lumpen males' which have been stressed in so many accounts of the skinhead phenomenon," wrote British author Dick Hebdige in *Subculture: The Meaning of Style*.

"Those values conventionally associated with white working-class culture which had been eroded by time, by relative affluence and by the disruption of the physical environment in which they had been rooted, were rediscovered embedded in black West Indian culture," Hebdige continued. "Here was a culture armoured against contaminating influences, protected against the more frontal assaults of the dominant ideology, denied access to the 'good life' by the color of its skin. Its rituals, language and style provided models for those white youths alienated from the parent culture by the imagined compromise of the post war years."

This was a pretty chancy alliance that needed continual monitoring. Solidarity was underscored by venting aggression on other, even more alien groups, such as homosexuals, hippies, and Asians. "Less easily assimilated than the West Indians into the host community," wrote Hebdige, "sharply differentiated not only by racial characteristics but by religious rituals, food taboos and a value system which encouraged deference, frugality and the profit motive, the Pakistanis were singled out for the brutal attentions of skinheads, black and white alike. Every time the boot went in, a contradiction was concealed, glossed over, made to 'disappear.' "

As the seventies wore on, and what was left of working-class society went down the drain in Britain, the skinheads — like most of the rest of youth culture — found themselves "boutiqued" past all meaning, marketed as a look, an attitude, or a sound that could be borrowed from or adulterated as part of a million different, personal styles. The threat of being co-opted by the larger culture accentuated the downwardly mobile, exaggeratedly proletarian tendencies among skinheads, reinforcing their chauvinism and puritanical rejection of consumerism. The more extreme expressions of skinhead disaffection, like slam-dancing and "Paki-bashing," assumed increased importance. And the one distinguishing mark of the skinhead vision — its mixture of immigrant and downscale white cultures — foundered, as any sense of interracial communality broke down. Without their dialogue with blacks, white skinheads, Hebdige writes, suddenly found themselves "sentenced to perpetual adolescence"—and, often, to White Power.

Time on the Cross

It should be pointed out that not all skinheads are Nazis, and a movement of skinheads in opposition to the Nazi model has asserted itself in recent years. Nevertheless, transplanted to the U.S., the Nazi skinheads have forged alliances with the Ku Klux Klan, and the racist majority of the skins has done more to popularize the far right than anything since the shootouts between the Order and the cops on the lonesome, survivalist plains of the new West.

In contrast to Britain and Western Europe, in America the skinheads are a suburban and small-town phenomenon. Although their class associations remain roughly intact, the less class-conscious American setting confers a more generalized, bully-boy air to skin rituals, and the deeper patterns of housing segregation in outlying areas make them far more vulnerable to separatist rhetoric. American skinheads are also often more purposefully violent.

The Anti-Defamation League (ADL), which has issued a series of detailed studies of the skinhead movement in the U.S., reported in 1989 that there were about 3,000 activist skinheads in thirty-one states, most of them concentrated in the West and, to a lesser extent, in the South. In

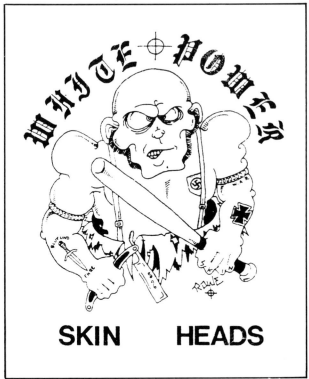

SKIN HEADS

WAR

Confederate Hammer

WAR

have been tied to forty crimes since 1987; they are known for activities like smearing "Hitler was Right," "Get out Jew Pig," and "Yahweh our White God" on synagogue walls. When a judge sentenced twenty-year-old Daniel Alvis Wood, a skin and a member of the KKK, to ten years in prison for these acts, Wood raised his arm in the Nazi salute.

In the Northwest, where Bob Mathews had wanted to set up his white bastion, skin violence became almost routine in the late eighties. Three Portland, Oregon skins beat an Ethiopian immigrant to death in November 1988. The Portland police said the city was experiencing six or seven skinhead crimes a week during March 1989.

Skinheads are fond of beating up people whom they think look gay or not white. In an interview, one member of the skinhead group American Front described how, in the spring of 1990, he and some friends nearly beat to death a young man, who was trying to get into the American Front:

> He invited himself to walk her home, then invited himself in, and then invited himself into her. I found this out a couple of days later. So I told a couple of my friends who had joined American Front little tidbits about him, bad points about him like how he's trying to get into American Front even though his name is Manuel. So we met him out of town, me and three other guys. We were playing on the swings and listening to Skrewdriver. I mean I wasn't even ready for it. He came down the sliding board, and they kicked him in the balls, [kicked] him really hard. And he's like, wait a minute what's going on. He ran down the hill, through a basketball court into a baseball field and stopped. He turned around and looked at us, thinking it was still joking around. Everybody jumped on him, beat the hell out of him. We got up and said take off your boots. He had one of 'em off in three seconds. We wanted his boots. That's the ultimate embarrassment. If you can't fight for your boots you don't deserve to wear them. We jumped on him again. Every-

California, the center of most skinhead activity, the ADL counted between thirty and forty activists in San Diego's WAR (White Aryan Resistance) Skins. Orange County, the Los Angeles suburb, had as many as 200 skins in ten different gangs, whose members drift from one community to another, hanging out on beaches or in shopping malls. Gang names change, but a 1989 list included the Orange County Skinheads, the Crazy Fuckin Skins, the Suicidals (a.k.a. The Boys), the Huntington Beach Hardcores, Evasive Action, FSU (Fuck Shit Up), the Northwest Orange County Skins, Huntington Beach Skins, the Peni Skins, and the WAR Skins.

In Texas, the Confederate Hammer Skins

WAR

body was kicking at his head. We had steel toes on. That was the nasty thing. And we all had fighting rings on. Everybody was hitting him or kicking him. One guy was kicking at his spine. Another guy hitting on the side of his face. Then I took my knife up the laces, and pulled the other boot off. He didn't move. He was unconscious. He was bleeding. Everybody had blood on their forearms. He seemed like a hemophiliac or something. We ran back up the hill laughing. One guy held up the boots because there was still a skin chick in the car. . . . He should have died. But he crawled to a house, just faintly knocked on the door. They came out to see what it was and got an ambulance. He lost so much blood he turned white. He got what he deserved.

Like most youth gangs, the skins place a very high value on conforming to the group consensus — as their boot-camp haircut and rolled jeans uniform suggests — and they reserve their most violent behavior for the fallen faithful.

Greg Withrow founded the White Student Union at American River College in Sacramento, California in 1979. Later, in an effort to tie his skins to former KKK grand dragon Tom Metzger's White Aryan Resistance, he added "Aryan Youth Movement" to its name.

But in 1987, Withrow found the love of a good woman, and under his girlfriend's influence he rejected his racist ways and went on television to denounce the racist movement. He announced plans to write an exposé. At that, Withrow's former colleagues broke into his apartment and beat him with baseball bats, stealing a copy of his manuscript as they departed. Later that summer, as Withrow was leaving his apartment to go for an evening walk, a blue pickup truck screeched to a halt alongside him and six members of the neo-Nazi group he had founded jumped out. They started beating and kicking Withrow. Dragging him into an empty lot, they tied his arms to a board. "They told me I was a traitor," he recalled, "and they held a gun to my head. Then they began to hammer nails in my hands. It seemed like they hammered forever, real slow. They told me they

American Front

American Front member Boyd Rice (left) and leader Bob Heick in San Francisco in 1989.

SYLVIA PLACHY

were doing it so I wouldn't write anymore."

Then one of his former colleagues pulled out a razor blade and cut a foot-long gash in Withrow's chest just below his neck. "That was so I wouldn't talk anymore," Withrow said.

Withrow passed out. On regaining consciousness some hours later, he managed to hobble down the street with the board still tied across his back, blood dripping from the nails in his palms. A white woman turned away when he appealed for help, as did a white couple he met a few steps further down the street. But a black couple emerging from a nightclub untied the gags in his mouth and called the police. "Ironic isn't it?" Withrow said later. "It was a black couple who finally rescued me." His experience only reinforced his determination to speak out against racism. "I want people to see that this is what I get because this is what I created. What goes around comes around."

Race Is the Reason

Withrow had been one of the bright lights of the revivified far-right movement that was taking shape under the direction of the gregarious, back-slapping Tom Metzger, a man you might easily mistake for a ward-heeling politician — if you didn't know he'd once been a head Kluxer. As the head of the 2,000-member White Aryan Resistance (WAR), Metzger is the single person most responsible for drawing young people into the far-right political movement, and his credentials are impeccable: He is the foremost West Coast Klan leader, a peer of far-right paragons Bob Miles and Richard Butler, and supposedly a recipient of some of the millions of dollars stolen by the Order. With the help of his son John, he has had remarkable success in recruiting a new skinhead youth wing. John Metzger became president of a WAR affiliate youth group called the Aryan Youth Movement (AYM) in 1987, when Greg Withrow renounced racism. Half of AYM's members are skinheads, and during the late 1980s it struck alliances with skin groups in San Francisco, Portland, Tulsa, Cincinnati, Detroit, New York, and Toronto.

Metzger has operated both through grassroots recruitment and through electoral campaigns. In a 1980 lecture, he said, "You don't make change having fiery crosses out in cow pastures. You make change by invading the halls of Congress and the Statehouse." In 1978, Metzger ran for San Diego County Supervisor; in 1980 he won the Democratic primary for Congress, but was overwhelmed in the general election. In 1982, he racked up more than 75,000 votes statewide in the race for the Democratic nomination for U.S. Senate.

Metzger ran the California branch of David Duke's Ku Klux Klan until he broke loose to form his own klavern in 1981. Where the diplomatic Duke is in the clutches of his nativist outriders on the further shores of the Republican Party, Metzger has embraced national socialism as if springtime for Hitler had finally sprung.

In an interview with me, Metzger explained his position:

I'm not a conservative really. In 1980 when I won the Democratic nomination [for Congress] and left the Klan, we had a meeting here on the West Coast and decided we would go a different direction. We decided we didn't need the ceremonial thing and we didn't need the right wing . . . I said, wait a minute. There's something wrong with my ideology. I'm in this right wing. I hear these guys saying let's nuke the Russians and things like that, and nuclear power is great and all this kind of stuff. And I started thinking. I said gee, you know, nuclear war is not good for the white race, and if there is nuclear war between the Soviet Union and the U.S., it will destroy the entire northern hemisphere which is the ancestral homeland of the Caucasian people. So what the hell am I doing saying whoopee let's nuke the Russians?

And then when I look on satellite TV and see the Russians and I see the majority of the people in European Russia are as white as anybody here, I say what the hell is this? It was illogical. So we moved towards going against the nuclear arms race, and armaments and war in general. Inside the country we believe in struggle. Outside the country, we took the position of self-determination of other races and other people. And for American corporations that betray the American worker and went to these places, what do we care if the self-determinists burn 'em out? . . .

And if the white man is going to survive, then we've got to have an ecology to survive in.

The government is going to want to take over more lands for military training. We find that to be a perfect issue for us. We don't want the environment to get any more messed up than it has to be and we don't want big brother to get any bigger.

We began to think a little broader and look into some of the left-wing positions, and we started evolving into something that can't be called right-wing. It can't be called Marxist and it's not really . . . The word populist has been ruined by the right wing, by the manipulations of [Willis Carto's] Populist Party. We don't accept that. We began to take on a lot of the positions of the left, and we started recruiting people from the left.

While Metzger acknowledges a certain respect for the National Front in Britain, he believes "they're too wrapped up in the Queen. That Queen worship stuff. I've told those people they've got

Current WAR leader Tom Metzger reading a California Ku Klux Klan newspaper, which he published, in 1980, when he was a prominent San Diego Klansmen.

Front page of a 1989 issue of Tom Metzger's White Aryan Resistance newspaper.

to become working-class revolutionary types and damn the Queen just like the left does, but do it from an honest position." But in general, the European right is both more diverse and less programmatic than the American scene, less obsessed with ideological purity, and that seems to suit Metzger's relaxed, California-style racism. "It's all very loose [in Europe], connections through friends, music and like that. There's no hard-core organization. The same ideas . . . We agree with Le Pen when Le Pen gets a big share of the Communist Workers vote there because of the third world workers coming into France. But when Le Pen pulls back to the old right-wing position and works with the conservatives, then we have a problem with him. They are a small percentage."

Metzger says he likes the far-right scene in America "*because* there is no center. It's all around but it's nowhere. It's like associations or networking. No fancy headquarters, or store fronts, or even book stores. Yet it's all over the place. A lot of times people are disappointed to come see Tom Metzger: they expect to see some sort of citadel, armed guards, barbed wire, and all that."

Metzger's own lower-key approach gives him more flexibility than other, more paramilitary groups on the American right:

Whenever we're able to recruit young people or change someone's way of thinking, young or old, we jump right in. If it were the Grey Panthers, it would be the same thing; wherever we see an opening, that's where we go. I am very pragmatic about everything. Wherever our opponents scream the loudest, that's where I go. They screamed about the skinheads. I've been trying to convince the skinheads to let their hair grow out and work into regular situations, melt into the public scene. A lot of them resisted that because they felt they had their fashion statement. Now the government is pushing them so hard they are being forced to do that. I'm basically an anti-system person. I enjoy that struggle, and how they go absolutely crazy. The big secret that they haven't rolled to is the left connection. We've already got left-wing papers screaming bloody murder about us. They are even having some introspection on how they missed the wagon with the blue collar white people — we read a lot of leftist papers. We're getting people who used to be SDS and stuff. The manag-

WAR Computer Bulletin Board

[Selected transcripts from the White Aryan Resistance "computer bulletin board," accessed by a network of members and supporters. Note: ZOG means "Zionist Occupation Government" (a.k.a. the United States government), and GFTT means "go for the throat."]

```
TITLE:   SEEKING A MATE
 FROM:   ██████████  (USER #7)
   TO:   WHT SINGLE WOMEN
 DATE:   APR-19-1986   TIME: 14:29:24.0
-----------------------------------------------------------------
```
Greetings, White Nationalist women. Are you 32-42, White and proud
of it, 5 ft. 7 in. or less? If so, I would like to meet you. I am
5 ft. 7 in. tall, have brown hair/hazel eyes, weigh 155 pounds, am
English/German bilingual. My hobbies are flags, music and sports.
I am looking for a down-to-earth lady who is not afraid to be a
White Nationalist. She should also be friendly, considerate, quiet
and gentle. One who is willing to work with her mate, in other
word, she should be a loyal, steadfast real sweetheart. I seek a
lady who has attributes similar to mine. Her weight must be in
proportion to her height. She can work, but she willing to stay
home 50 percent of the time. Any job is fine, especially a flight
attendant. I consider them to be excellently trained to be good
wives and mothers. . . . As to her religion? Catholic, Protestant,
Identity, Klan, Mormon, Nazi, Odinist is OK to me.

```
TITLE:   KILLING
 FROM:   ██████████  (USER #1)
   TO:   KINSMEN
 DATE:   MAY-24-1986   TIME: 17:15:11.7
-----------------------------------------------------------------
```
   Let's get serious now folks. The fact is that the only way to
be free of what threatens you is to kill it. So learn to kill.
Quickly. Quietly. Without witnesses.
   A very neat trick is to loosen the fittings to a car's master
cylinder so there is a gradual loss of brake fluid as the brakes
are used. Finally resulting in no brakes and a lot of unchecked
inertia.
   Another prank is to burn a ZOG newspaper in your adversary's
home. You must use some technique though. Cover the floor with one
thickness of the unfolded paper, then light it. It causes a
surprising amount of damage.
   The old standby is to drill a small hole in his lightbulb and
fill it with gunpowder. When the light goes on, he goes out. GFTT.

Aryan Youth Movement leader John Metzger looks on as a Nazi skinhead hangs a WAR banner in 1989.

ing editor of my paper is an ex-Trotskyite; one of my main writers is John Jewel, who was on the executive board of the IWW up in Canada and fought in the streets as a flaming left-winger during the Vietnam War. . . . We've also made dents with the Earth First movement [a group of ecologi-

cal radicals known for spiking trees marked by lumber companies and threatening to destroy power lines], the ecology situation, animal rights. The head of our Aryan Women's League wrote an article about saving the wolves . . . we're definitely left of center with a racial concept, racial separatism. And we feel our number one enemy is within our own race.

We re-identified who the enemy is. The right wing, being used pretty much by the conservative movement, the Republicans, was always pointing at the blacks or the Jews. . . . We said wait a minute. Most of the guys in the government are white. They're not Jews. They're not black. So who's screwing us? It's our own people. So we said, well, we got to divide them, what are they and what are we. They're economic determinists. We're racial and cultural determinists. So essentially we're in a protracted civil war among white people.

All the other races are a side issue. That's when I began to have meetings with Farrakhan and all these people. Since it is good that central power be weakened and split up, maybe there's a chance outside of government to have meetings with peoples of other races about splitting up geography in a real idea of separatist states. We've pushed that for some time. . . . We've picked up on the old Wobbly struggles, Eugene Debs and Jack London and this kind of stuff, and began to reformulate new heroes for our racial struggle. That's brought us into confrontation with the old right. Some of them call us Bolsheviks. The Marxists call us Nazis and fascists.

Metzger is especially comfortable discussing the early, formative days of the National Socialist movement, which also exhibited a mix of left- and right-wing thought:

It was not to be a world conqueror–type thing. It was to be an internal revolution. . . . It's too bad the Libertarians can't come to grips with the race issue, because if they could, the anarcho-Libertarians would be very attractive. But they will not allow the concept of race into their thinking. We're not saying race is everything, but we're saying you cannot think of things without race.

We have Christian Identity people in our association, but we won't allow any kind of religious ideas to take over the organization. We have

some pretty tough arguments about that. I used to be Christian Identity, but I'm an atheist now. I just don't believe it. On the other hand, there are a lot of good people who I don't want to run off that *do* have that feeling. We can argue about that over a beer any time. But I find a problem in dealing with religious-oriented people. They are very doctrinaire and they like to push their way too hard.

Metzger agreed that his operation had both

an above- and a below-ground operation:

To a degree. You've got a lot of closet-oriented people. You've got survivalists. You've got people who agree with you on some things, but not all things. It's not rigid at all; it's not good to be rigid now. You'd just be a target. So when the system punches it, it's like punching cotton. They might get a couple, but they don't get everybody.

When we shifted gears in 1980, the press took the signal that there was a lot less people in the right wing conservative movement. And they were right. We were shifting to a new ideology. Bob Miles knows this. He knew what I was doing all the way along. Some of the old reactionary types couldn't keep up. When I began to work with the National Front and the Australian Workers Party, and even with people in Eastern Europe, they just didn't quite understand. When I attacked the system, whether it be [ultra-conservative commentator] Pat Buchanan or whoever it might be, the reverberations began . . . what the hell is this guy doing?

It's a life force. Some people could call it a subculture. It changes. There's a real right wing and a real left wing to it. We never could have won with these right wing conservatives. That has been a losing position. It's been the boss man's position. It's been a loser. It's strange because the racial movement used to be more to the left, with people like [Jack] London who said, "I'm a socialist, a party man. But number one I'm a white working man." Somewhere it got off the track and was co-opted by the conservatives. What I'm trying to do is retrace our steps somewhat and get it back on the track and attack the conservatives and drive them out.

As in any movement, the small organizations that populate the far right come and go, changing their names, moving across the country, keeping in touch by video and audio cassettes. The Bible study groups in Nebraska and Kansas that periodically gathered to listen to Jim Wickstrom's Posse tapes expanded to the air waves, as in Dodge City, where KTTL, under the direction of Charles and Nellie Babs, broadcasts Christian Identity news across the Midwest. Today, Tom Metzger's weekly television show, *Race and Reason*, purports to reach nearly fifty different cable markets.

**Miracle
Whip
Kultur**

Miracle Whip Kultur

It has been commonplace to dismiss the clandestine activities of the Klan, Aryan Nations, and other racialist far-right groups as isolated occurrences on the fringes of society, and to write off their members as lunatic extremists with little chance of gaining anything more than a fragile foothold on power and influence in a supposedly egalitarian society. But increasingly, race seems to lie just below the surface of nearly every political debate, and the opinions of the extreme right have been voiced by mainstream figures on both the political and cultural scenes, as ever more visible signs of interracial hostility have emerged. Since the early 1980s, especially, the parameters of acceptable discourse and behavior have broadened, making room for more and more openly racialist viewpoints.

Smashing Taboos

"There is no place in the party of Abraham Lincoln and George Bush for a hatemonger like [David] Duke. . . . Let me repeat: racism has no place in America, and for that same reason, David Duke has no place in the Republican Party,"

National Republican Committee Chairman Lee Atwater told the *Boston Globe* during Duke's run for the Louisiana legislature on the Republican ticket.

This was the same Atwater who in the fall of 1988, as George Bush's presidential campaign manager, had helped to engineer one of the most successful media campaigns in recent political history, with race at its foundation. Atwater took the lackluster Bush and transformed him into a tough-but-kindly American candidate, at the same time playing on racist sentiments in portraying Bush's opponent, Michael Dukakis, as the wimpy dupe of an evil black rapist and murderer, Willie Horton — a criminal whom Dukakis had supposedly let out of jail temporarily on a furlough program.

But that's business as usual. When it comes to race in America, there have always been two sets of books: one for the public in which any suggestion of race is omitted, and a surreptitious second ledger where race is part and parcel of everyday life.

National figures like Atwater and David Duke have been careful to publicly distance themselves from the organizations of the far right. Characteristic of this discretion is a statement that Duke himself made in the *New York Times* in June 1990. "There are many liberals today who were radical leftists in their younger days. I'm a conservative who might have been considered a radical rightist in my younger days," said the former grand wizard of the Louisiana Knights of the Ku Klux Klan.

In offering such reassurance Duke pays homage to the I'm-no-extremist-I'm-just-like-you requirements of discussing race as a politician who needs to seek majority appeal. But many figures in entertainment or the media are not bound by such constraints; they are able to survive or even take advantage of the increased attention from one-time

flaps, furors, and outrages, which translate racial criticisms into incendiary media events. In fact, in a time of broadcast and print information overload, there's nothing like a taboo to cut through the clutter and get noticed.

Two such figures in popular music who were recently at such flash points of controversy were Richard (Professor Griff) Griffin of the rap group Public Enemy, and Axl Rose of Guns N' Roses. Professor Griff, Public Enemy's "Minister of Information" drew fire when he was quoted in a May 1988 article in the *Washington Times* as saying "Jews are wicked . . . [and responsible for] the majority of wickedness that goes on across the globe." He went on to say that they financed the slave trade and are "responsible for what's happening in South Africa." He also wondered if it was "a coincidence that the Jews run the jewelry business and it's named jewelry."

In the wake of these remarks, Public Enemy's leader, Carlton (Chuck D.) Ridenhour announced that Professor Griff was no longer a member of the group. He was replaced by Harry Allen, who has himself gone on record expressing belief in a theory that all races derive from the black race as a result of experimental grafting and that light pigmentation is a mark of genetic inferiority, which explains the insecurity that fuels whites' need to hold the black man down.

Rose, lead singer and songwriter of Guns N' Roses, a band whose first album sold nine million copies, stirred criticism when he wrote and recorded such lyrics as "Immigrants and faggots . . . come to our country/And think they'll do as they please . . . Police and niggers get out of my way/I don't need to buy none of your gold chains today" on their album *One in A Million*. In defending his choice of words in an interview with *Rolling Stone* magazine, Rose said, "Why can black people go up to each other and use the word 'nigger,' but when a white guy does it, all of a sudden it's a big put down. . . . I use the word 'nigger' to describe somebody that is a pain in your life, a problem. The word 'nigger' doesn't necessarily mean black."

To some, the emergence of musical groups expressing blatant racialism signifies a new, racially

We're TAKING it back!

WHITE ARYAN RESISTANCE

WAR

"THE LAST FULL MEASURE!"

Participants in a 1989 Labor Day rally in Gainesville, Georgia.

polarized climate in the country, a transition from covert to overt hostility.

"In the past year," wrote Dave Marsh in the May 1990 issue of *Playboy*, "rock's *Ebony and Ivory* dream has exploded as overt racism rushed far past the exhortations of neofacist skinheads at the postpunk fringe into the scene's central currents. . . . Guns N' Roses and Public Enemy [weren't] just another bad boy pose. It's for real, an unfolding of the endemic segregation at the heart of the day-to-day business of the music world. What's new is that, in the aftermath of the affirmative-action era, hardly anyone is even pausing to apologize for making big bucks off bigotry."

Similar developments have occurred among comedians, where sudden popularity is often a register of attitude changes in the public mind.

Traditionally, stand-up comics have relied on the tensions created by an ethnic identity for humor. But in contrast to the cross-cultural appeal of Richard Pryor and his live concert films, which affirmed black identity without virulently attacking anyone, or the world weary wisecracks of old-line Borscht Belt comedians like Myron Cohen, the late 1980s brought such performers as Andrew Dice Clay.

Clay, a stand-up arena concert comedian, spews racist and sexist lines from an Elvis-is-alive-and-living-in-Bensonhurst pose. At his shows, young men in the audience stand up and cheer — with what seems to be a powerful feeling of release —as his comic alter-ego allows Clay to voice anger and ideas repressed by public taboos.

The Fringe Becomes Part of the Fabric

The trend of increased tolerance for figures with strong racial views may well have signalled a change in how open racial conflict may now become, a change also evident in the upsurge in reported incidents of race-related violence.

In New York City in the spring of 1990, newspapers and broadcasts were dominated by accounts of the Brooklyn trials of Keith Mondello and Joey Fama, accused of being leader and trigger-man in a fatal street mob attack on a young black man, Yusef Hawkins. Tensions from the incident and from a highly publicized boycott of a Korean grocery by black protesters reached the point where Mayor David Dinkins felt the need to make an address to the city pleading for calm.

While such episodes erupted spontaneously in America's cities, there was also evidence that the organized groups on the racist far right were alive and well in the 1990s. In Georgia, the Center

AT&T Shareholders Vote on Racism

[On April 18, 1990, at the AT&T Annual Meeting, the following anti-affirmative action proposal submitted by William Pierce's National Alliance received nine percent of the vote—one percentage point more than a similar proposal submitted in 1989.]

Shareholder Proposal 3:

The National Alliance, Post Office Box 2264, Arlington, VA 22202, has submitted the following proposal:

"WHEREAS, so-called 'Affirmative Action' programs developed to recruit, employ and promote qualified non-Whites may contribute toward discrimination against qualified White employees and job applicants;

"WHEREAS, AT&T has developed an extensive Affirmative Action Program to recruit, employ and promote qualified non-Whites; therefore, be it

"RESOLVED, that the shareholders of AT&T hereby request the Board of Directors to take the necessary steps to phase out those aspects of AT&T's Affirmative Action Program which are directed toward recruiting, employing or promoting individuals from any particular racial or ethnic group."

Supporting Statement

"Dear Fellow Shareholder,

DID YOU KNOW that James J. Meenan, Corporate Vice President, told a meeting of Black employees on December 14, 1988 that a special 'Action Committee' had been formed whose initiatives were 'establishing summer internship programs for *minority* secondary school students, achieving 50% *minority representation* in college internship and summer hire programs and establishing interactive relationships with colleges have *large minority populations* and with *minority-focused* community and professional organizations.' (Emphasis added.) Is this fair to White students and job applicants? Is this what our Company means when it claims that the objective of its Affirmative Action Program is 'to provide *equal* opportunity for *all*'?

"DID YOU KNOW that according to a recent Gallup poll conducted for *Newsweek* magazine, which was reported in its March 7, 1988 issue, 80% of the Whites, as well as 50% of the Blacks who were polled, felt that 'qualified blacks should not receive preference over equally qualified whites in such matters as getting into college or getting jobs.'

"DID YOU KNOW that although Blacks represent 11.9% of the U.S. population, *over 14%* of AT&T employees are Black? Is *more* 'Affirmative Action' really necessary?

"It has been claimed that an Affirmative Action Program for non-Whites is required for AT&T to remain a federal contractor and subcontractor, and to qualify for certain state and municipal government business. Yet, according to information contained in the *1988 Proxy Statement*, 'AT&T's total business in 1986 with the Federal Government represented about 6% of total revenues.'

"If you agree that those aspects of AT&T's so-called 'Affirmative Action' Program which are based on one's racial or ethnic group should be phased out, please be sure to mark your proxy card with an 'X' in the FOR box associated with this proposal. If you leave the boxes for this proposal unmarked on your proxy card, your shares will automatically be voted against this proposal. Remember, no matter how few or how many shares you own, *every vote counts!*"

for Democratic Renewal brought a civil suit against the fire department of Blakely, a small town in the southwestern part of the state. The Center charged that the department provided "unequal" protection in fighting fires in homes of black people because its chief was a member of the Ku Klux Klan, and the department answered to the Klan's dictates rather than those of public service. "For two hours after the fire truck and crew arrived I stood by helplessly and watched as the fire continued to blaze up, sending sparks up over our own home with each wind shift," one resident said. "Water was applied for about five minutes at the very beginning. After two hours more water was applied. . . . A member of the fire department said they wanted the fire to 'just burn out by itself' and that they decided to 'help beautify the street.' " The fire department's actions resulted in the deaths of two children, one of whom, according to the suit, was hosed down at the fire scene while he was covered with severe burns. In bringing the suit, C.T. Vivian, chairman of the Center for Democratic Renewal, pointed out it was "a tragic and fantastic irony" to discover the Klan operating an arm of government in 1990, on the twenty-fifth anniversary of the passage of the 1964 Civil Rights Act.

Also in 1990, Ralph Forbes, the Christian Identity minister, former George Lincoln Rockwell lieutenant, and 1989 campaign manager for David Duke, scored a spectacular, if brief, victory in his primary run for lieutenant governor of Arkansas, before losing the run-off election. In Arizona, Evan Mecham, the far-right governor, once surrounded by Posse-style assistants, was forced out of office as a result of impeachment; but in 1990 he bounced back, running in the Republican gubernatorial primary.

And on the fringes, the Posse Comitatus, which had all but disappeared since the mid-1980s, emerged once again, sponsoring training seminars in Idaho and North Carolina. In the spring of 1990 the FBI arrested two Aryan Nations members in a plot to bomb Seattle's largest gay nightclub. They also had targeted Korean-owned businesses and bars patronized by a largely black clientele in nearby Tacoma. Skinheads also began to single out Asians along with gays in their street attacks.

The numbers of these different groups are difficult to estimate; but there are a few general guideposts. One of the most popular publications of the movement, the *Spotlight*, maintained a circulation of 100,000 during the 1980s. David Duke drew 44,000 votes in his presidential campaign, and in his 1990 Senate campaign he had built a mailing list of upwards of 30,000. Another way of determining the strength of the movement lies in the numbers of people who refused to pay taxes. According to figures cited by James Coates in his book *Armed and Dangerous*, the IRS found 17,222 Posse tax protesters in 1980. By 1983 that number had grown to 57,754, and still remained at approximately 52,000 in 1986. The IRS took the matter seriously enough to assign 200 auditors to Posse cases.

Many of these white supremacist groups have adapted their roles, methods, and activities to the atmosphere of more open racialism in mainstream society. Since the Klan's eclipse in the 1960s, its symbols have worked their way into an ever-wider circle of American culture, where they have been shorn of their frightening history, becoming staple images in film and on television. The spooky mysteries of Klan culture have been largely demystified: If cross-burnings once were scary rites conducted deep in dark, echoing southern woods, they now happen on suburban front lawns and flood into millions of homes via Madonna videos.

The Ku Klux Klan protests Martin Luther King Day in Pulaski, Tennessee on January 13, 1990.

As the nation's laws turned against the Klan in the 1920s, individual states passed anti-masking laws to prevent the hooded terrorists from so easily engaging in their vigilante activities. In the spring of 1990, a Georgia judge ruled the Klan had the right to wear masks, but by this time, the organization's strategies made masks a relic of the past. Their former Louisiana grand wizard David Duke, now a candidate for the U.S. Senate, was appearing as a formidable electoral candidate in a suit and tie on *Nightline.*

And while Duke's candidacy is a particularly

overt example of the influx of far-right thinking into mainstream politics, it also reflects a growing national trend. As Louisiana Governor Buddy Roemer points out: "You can't come down here and say that Louisiana has a problem that's different than anyone else's. We have a mouth that's different but not a problem."

There are any number of factors contributing to this change in the character of public life, which is bringing racism further and further out of the closet. One of the most influential was the nod and wink given the far right by the Reagan government. Ronald Reagan played to the romantic past of small-town America, invoking the cultural symbolism that was so important to Barry Goldwater's supporters, and later to the followers of George Wallace. It was more of a reminiscence of a nativist past than a stirring new call for action. But it signalled a new tolerance for racialist attitudes and politics at the highest levels of government.

The most dramatic legacy of the Reagan era has been its institutionalization of his brand of conservatism, in which the remnants of the New Deal and welfare statism were replaced with free-market economics, government deregulation of business, and the abandonment of attempts to promote social equality or to guarantee adequate provision of employment, housing, nutrition, health care, education, or income. The administration's argument was that egalitarianism and redistribution of wealth led to a static, even depressed, economy. Inequality was a requisite result of sound economic growth, and the wealth created by the rich would lift up the poor as well, by way of a "trickle down." By the end of the 1980s, Social Darwinism was the accepted theory in Washington.

This new doctrine of inequality provided a rationalization for the deep racial splits in American society. In the 1980s, the black family median income was 56 percent of the income of white families. More than a third of all blacks and a quarter of Hispanics lived below the poverty line. Living patterns in most cities continued to be determined by race. Segregation was the rule, not the exception, and a study by the Southern Poverty Law Center concluded that most outbursts of racial violence occurred as a feature of segregated housing. The percentage of blacks going to college began declining. The rich were getting richer and an ever-increasing number of poor people of all races were growing poorer. As of 1987, 15 percent of white children lived below the poverty level, along with 45 percent of black children and 39 percent of Hispanic children.

In the last decade, the frustrations of the growing ranks of undereducated, underemployed white youths faced with a declining industrial workplace and a perceptibly eroding social status have also fueled racial hostility. It has been precisely kids' need to act out — the need to establish a social identity — that makes them so useful to racialist revolutionaries, and prime for recruitment by movements like the skinheads. Both the rightist ("Extremism in pursuit of virtue is no vice") and the rocker ("Too Much Ain't Enough") ethos embody a certain recklessness that feeds on the outrage it provokes from the larger culture. Motivated youth are invaluable to any political movement, and the far right are able to attract them in numbers. As Nazi leader Harold Covington said, "One long-haired, dope-smoking, rock and roll freak who will act is worth more [to a political movement] than a thousand blond-haired, blue-eyed purists who sit in their goddamned armchairs and criticize!"

The far right also found a home amidst the economic dislocations of the farm crisis. Populists and liberals had for decades waged unsuccessful

White power T-shirts on display at a gathering of the racist far right in 1986.

CHARLIE ARNOT

attacks on American finance as an inequitable system under which the government gave up its prerogatives to manage the nation's finances to a private Federal Reserve System. Those attacks gained new currency in the 1980s when they were brought into the farm belt by the far right, albeit always as part of an attack on the worldwide Jewish conspiracy. (In fact, Jews do not manage or own any of the large international banking concerns.) Liberals and progressives during the 1960s had argued for empowerment of the poor, working to pass legislation providing them with the right to lawyers and access to the court system. But in the farm crisis, with plenty of evidence of an unjust farm credit system and unfair foreclosure practices by both private banks and the federal government, liberals and conservatives alike stood mute. It was the racist far right that counselled farmers to fight back by going to court, facing judges, and arguing their cases on their own, and that urged them to intro-

duce harassing and oftentimes far-fetched legal defenses aimed not so much at winning but at providing time to negotiate and stall in the face of foreclosure. And it was the far right that first introduced an overall analysis of the rural depression that provided thousands of displaced people with an explanation of events affecting their own lives, making them something other than guilty victims.

The existence of the income tax, which the far right has long argued is unconstitutional and an infringement on its sometimes cockeyed notion of a republic, has long been a staple issue. By the 1980s the IRS was reporting the existence of tens of thousands of Posse-minded tax protesters. It was tax protest that got Gordon Kahl into trouble with the law; the shootout with federal marshals and the manhunt across the Midwest assured him the status of martyr. Order leader Bob Mathews also had his first brush with the law by refusing to file income taxes. First broached by the far right, the idea of unfair taxes and individual action to protest them gradually filtered into the mainstream right wing. In the 1970s the Jarvis-Gans protest movement in California formed the crest of a national movement against taxation and provided one of the sturdiest planks of Reagan's first campaign for the presidency.

Anti-alienism also remained an active motif in American politics in the 1980s. The debate over illegal aliens became a centerpiece of national politics as the Congress debated over new immigration legislation, and the "English Only" movement to delegitimize the use of foreign languages won widespread support. In 1988 the Democratic Party, which since the New Deal era had promoted the reduction of barriers to international trade, began to adopt protectionist positions amidst a xenophobic atmosphere that featured autoworkers bashing Japanese cars with sledgehammers. By 1990, nationalist attacks on aliens were taking place across much of the western world, with West Germans attacking Turkish workers, angry French supporting far-right politicians against North Africans, and British skinheads going out Paki-bashing. And in newly free-marketized Eastern Europe, there were signs of a resurgence of the open anti-Semitism which had been stifled during the years of communist rule.

The Red Scare and the White Scare

The threat of the alien, so often linked with the campaign against radicals and communists, has always been a durable theme in American politics, but with the election of Ronald Reagan, this theme took on new coloration. It lay at the heart of the new Reagan doctrine — that collection of policies and strategies that created a revolution in right-wing thinking about anticommunism. Basically the Reagan doctrine presented the idea of fighting the Soviet empire on its periphery in the Third World instead of retreating into a fortress-like America to fend off foreign entanglements. Nowhere was that struggle more emphasized than in Central America, where the U.S. had conceded its customary foothold, the Panama Canal, and where (the Reaganites argued) the Soviets would set off on a march up through the soft underbelly of Mexico into the United States itself. In an episode reminiscent of Posse fantasies, Reagan went on television to warn of the sinister possibilities of Soviet surrogates worming their way across the border, disguised as Mexican laborers. And the investigation into the Iran/Contra scandal revealed that Oliver North had routinely used the threat of Soviet aircraft taking off and landing in Nicaragua as part

of his pitch to raise money for the president's not-so-secret funding of the Contras.

Such fears formed the basis for the more aggressive domestic intervention by the Federal Bureau of Investigation, whose surveillance and harassment of radicals had supposedly been curtailed in the 1970s by the Church Committee's Senate investigations into the misuse of covert operations by intelligence agencies. In the 1980s, the FBI undertook a broad new inquiry into groups that opposed American foreign policy in El Salvador, Nicaragua, and Guatemala. By mid-decade, the Bureau had gathered files on dozens of peace groups, placed an unknown number under surveillance, and employed informants to infiltrate and disrupt the activities of leading groups. Frank Varelli, one FBI informant, made dossiers on prominent American politicians, including members of Congress. He established a back channel between the FBI and death squads in El Salvador, who were alerted to the imminent arrivals of visiting American liberals.

So while anticommunism did not reverberate in the same way as it had in the 1950s, it nonetheless provided the centerpiece of Reagan's foreign policy. In addition, it bound together the factions of the emerging New Right, which otherwise would have opposed one another. The older, big-business-and-defense-oriented conservatives were thus linked to the new socially oriented conservatives and to the Cold War neoconservatives.

Meanwhile, race itself remained a durable staple on the domestic political scene. In the 1988 presidential campaign, Jesse Jackson's candidacy split the Democratic Party along racial lines, and his campaign was ultimately crushed in New York under the sharp and racially grounded attack of the then-mayor, Ed Koch. George Bush's campaign employed race as a major drawing card for southern white voters who were leaving the Democratic Party. In addition to his race-based Willie Horton ads, Bush's campaign was redolent with xenophobic imagery. From the flag to the Pledge of Allegiance, he portrayed himself as a super-patriot. The nostalgia for a nativist past became the dominant motif in the Connecticut blue blood's successful campaign for president. The far right — nativist rear guard that it was — had exercised an extraordinary role in creating the symbolism of modern American life.

As the rapid vaporization of the Soviet Union as an expansionist power has deprived the right wing of a reliable bogeyman, it has actually made race seem more of a social insignia than ever — so much so that a TV commercial for a new line of "Soviet" jeans actually depicts the Russian language serving as a humanizing bridge between a pair of black youths and a pair of Bensonhurst-type white teens.

In fact, as the communist threat diminishes, race grows ever-larger as a principle of social organization in most areas of public life, and race-related issues dominate the political arena: Should English remain the official language in all areas of the country as we enter the next century? Will the "war on drugs" replace the war on communism — and haven't blacks and Hispanics already become the chief targets of that war? As national structures disintegrate to make way for a single world economy, how will minorities express significant political leverage? Black men in Harlem already have a lower life expectancy than men in Bangladesh, yet most of Congress is busy weighing aid proposals for Eastern Europe, not 125th Street.

With political change sweeping across the world, and American society once again undergoing a period of social flux, race, almost by default, defines the social contours of society. And because it does, the far-right political cadres receive a fresh breath of life and remain, as they always have been, a constant factor in the nation's life.

My man is a White racist. If yours is a whimp, dump him and get a real White man and screw the system

Bibliographic Notes

Bibliographic Notes

Introduction: Tight, Right, and White

For a general discussion of American nativism, see John Higham's classic *Strangers in the Land* (New Brunswick: Rutgers University Press, 1963) and David H. Bennett's *The Party of Fear* (Chapel Hill: University of North Carolina, 1988). The latter provides an excellent resume of the far-right groups active during the 1980s. Also of interest is *The Paranoid Style in American Politics and Other Essays*, by Richard Hofstadter (University of Chicago, 1979)

For detailed accounts of the far right in the 1980s, see "The Far Right," by Leonard Zeskind, in *Schmate* (Summer 1985); *Hate, Violence and White Supremacy: A Decade Review, 1980-1990*, a report by the Southern Poverty Law Center's Klanwatch project (Montgomery, Alabama, 1989); and *They Don't All Wear Sheets: A Chronology of Racist and Far Right Violence, 1980-1986*, compiled by Chris Lutz, published by the Center for Democratic Renewal (Atlanta, 1987).

Chapter 1: The Worldwide Conspiracy

Norman Cohn provides an excellent, detailed account of the myth of the Jew as demon and the history and spread of the *Protocols* in *Warrant for Genocide* (New York: Harper & Row, 1969). Excerpts from the *Protocols* are taken from the version entitled *The Protocols of the Meetings of the Learned Elders of Zion*, translated from the Russian by Victor E. Marsden. Henry Ford's compilation of the *Dearborn Independent* articles is from *The International Jew: The World's Foremost Problem*, by Henry Ford, Sr., abridged (London: no publisher listed, 1948).

For the history of the Ku Klux Klan, see *The Fiery Cross: The Ku Klux Klan in America*, by Wyn Craig Wade (New York: Simon & Schuster, 1987); and *Hooded Americanism: The History of the Ku Klux Klan*, by David M. Chambers (Durham, N.C.: Duke University Press, 1989). For accounts of the far right between the two world wars, see *Voices of Protest: Huey Long, Father Coughlin & the Great Depression*, by Alan Brinkley (New York: Random House, 1982); "Henry Ford and the International Jew," by Leo P. Ribuffo, in *American Jewish History*, Vol. LXIX, No. 4 (June 1980); and *The Old Christian*

Right: The Protestant Far Right from the Great Depression to the Cold War, by Leo P. Ribuffo (Philadelphia: Temple University Press, 1983). For Christian Identity history, see *These Also Believe*, by Charles S. Braden (New York: Macmillan, 1949), and *The Heritage of the Anglo-Saxon Race*, by M.H. Gayer (Haverhill, Mass.: Destiny Publishers, 1941). Timothy P. Weber provides an excellent analysis of recent trends in the fundamentalist movement in *Living in the Shadow of the Second Coming: American Premillenialism, 1875-1982* (Grand Rapids, Mich: Zondervan Corp., 1983).

Chapter 2: Resurgence

For background on the John Birch Society, see "The John Birch Society," in *Facts*, published by the Anti-Defamation League (February 1966). For information on the Minutemen, see "The Minutemen: Spirit of '66," by William W. Turner, in *Ramparts* (January 1967); and *The Minutemen, America's Last Line of Defense Against Communism*, published by the Minutemen (Norborne, Missouri, undated). For more on George Lincoln Rockwell, see *American Swastika*, by Charles Higham (New York: Doubleday, 1985); and for the U.S. Neo-Nazi movement, see *Facts* (March 1978); and "Racist Leader Could Be Nasty, Charming . . . or Pitiful," by Hank Burchard, in the *Washington Post* (August 26, 1967).

For background on Carto and the Liberty Lobby, see *The Liberty Lobby & the American Right*, by Frank P. Mintz (Westport, Conn.: Greenwood Press, 1985); "The Strange Story of Willis Carto," By C.H. Simonds, in the *National Review* (September 10, 1971); *Looking Forward: A Study of the New Trend within the Conservative Movement*, published by the Liberty Lobby (Washington, D.C., 1965); and *Profiles in Populism*, edited by Willis A. Carto (Liberty Lobby, 1982).

For an early history of the FBI, see Max Lowenthal's *The Federal Bureau of Investigation* (New York: William Sloane, 1950). *The FBI & Martin Luther King* by David Garrow (New York: W.W. Norton & Co., 1981) includes a detailed account of the Bureau's spying on King. *The Age of Surveillance*, by Frank G. Donner (New York: Alfred A. Knopf, 1980) is full of rich insights into the operation of the police and their relationship to the state. For more on the resurgence of the Klan, see *The True Story of the Ku Klux Klan vs. Organized Labor*, by Paul and Trisha McLennan with David Chambers (Atlanta: Center for Democratic Renewal, 1985).

Chapter 3: The Fifth Era

Various accounts of the armed underground Order have been written over the last decade. Chief among them are *The Silent Brotherhood: Inside America's Racist Underground*, by Kevin Flynn and Gary Gerhardt (New York: Free Press, 1989); and *Armed and Dangerous, the Rise of the Survivalist Right*, by James Coates (New York: Hill & Wang, 1987).

Chapter 4: Posse Country

Leonard Zeskind of the Center for Democratic Renewal is a rich source of information on the Posse. In-depth information on Gordon Kahl and the Posse can also be found in *Bitter Harvest: Gordon Kahl and the Posse Comitatus: Murder in the Heartland*, by James Corcoran (New York: Viking Penguin, 1990). For background on Henry Beach see *The Oregonian* (June 23, 1985). Bruce Maxwell wrote a comprehensive series of articles on Posse-style extremists, published in the *Rochester* [Minnesota] *Post-Bulletin* during November of 1984.

The account of events at the Rulo farm is based on my own reporting, much of which first appeared in the *Village Voice* in 1985. Some information about the murders comes from an interview with Mike Ryan, conducted by me and my film colleagues Kevin Rafferty, Charlie Arnot, and Anne Bohlen, on death row at the Nebraska state penitentiary in Lincoln in 1986. Lester Gibson and Denny Whelan also helped to explain the case.

Chapter 5: New White Politics

For an extensive and informative treatment of David Duke's life and times see *The Klan*, by Patsy Sims (New York: Stein & Day, 1978). Jerry Thompson, Robert Sherborne, and Susan Thomas wrote about Bill Wilkinson's role as an FBI informant in the *Tennessean* (August 30, 1981). Lance Hill and the Louisiana Coalition against Racism & Nazism have published collections of local newspaper and magazine articles about Duke and excerpts from his various writings, along with Abby Kaplan's 1989 interview with Duke: see their report *The Politics and Background of State Representative David Duke* (New Orleans, 1990). More information on Duke can also be found in *Ballot Box Bigotry: David Duke and the Populist Party*, the Center for Democratic Renewal's Background Report #7 (Atlanta, 1989).

For the history of the international skinhead movement and its political and cultural roots, see *Subculture: The Meaning of Style*, by Dick Hebdige (London: Methuen, 1979); and *Skinhead*, by Nick Knight (London: Omnibus, 1982). The most comprehensive ongoing account of the international far-right movement is contained in *Searchlight* magazine, published monthly in London. Especially informative are the *Searchlight* articles "Nazism: A Specter Haunting Europe for 1990" (January 1990), "From a Poisoned Well" (October 1989), and "From Ballots to Bombs: The Inside Story of the National Front's Political Soldiers" (1989). For more on the revival of nationalism and the resulting wave of anti-Semitism and other racist tendencies, see "The Long Shadow," in *Newsweek* (May 7, 1990).

Greg Withrow's ordeal was described in "Ex-Racist Says He Was Crucified for Changing Views," an unsigned dispatch from Knight-Ridder published in the *Atlanta Constitution* (August 12, 1987). For details on the evolution of the skinhead-Klan alliance see "Skinhead Nation," by Jeff Coplon, in *Rolling Stone* (December 1, 1986). The Anti-Defamation League has also published a series of detailed reports on the skinhead movement: see "Shaved for Battle" (1987), "Young and Violent" (1988), "The Skinheads: Update" (1988), and "Skinheads Target the Schools" (1989).

Tom Metzger's views are regularly presented on his cable television show, "Race and Reason." His comments in this book come from my own interview with him in June 1989 in Fallbrook, California, and from subsequent telephone updates.

Epilogue: Miracle Whip Kultur.

For Axl Rose's views on race see "The Rolling Stone Interview with Axl Rose," by Del James, in *Rolling Stone* (August 10, 1989). Dave Marsh's views on the racist nature of the music business come from his article "Rocking Racism," in Playboy (March 1990).

For data on and analysis of the growing gap between rich and poor, black and white, see *Terror in Our Neighborhoods: A Report on Housing Violence*, published by the Southern Poverty Law Center (Montgomery, Alabama, April 1990).

For an overview of white student groups, see "America's Youthful Bigots," by Art Levine, in *US News & World Report* (May 7, 1990); "Campus Ethnoviolence," Report #4 of the National Institute Against Prejudice & Violence (Baltimore, March 1990); and "The Colleges: Fear, Loathing & Suppression," by Nat Hentoff, in the *Village Voice* (May 8, 1990).

INDEX

INDEX